Mossymere

Mossymere

John Bailey

The Crowood Press

First published in 1988 by
The Crowood Press
Ramsbury, Marlborough
Wiltshire SN8 2HE

British Library Cataloguing in Publication Data

Bailey, John
Mossymere.
I. Title
823'.914 F

ISBN 0 946284 04 0

Typeset by Alacrity Phototypesetters
Banwell Castle, Weston-super-Mare
Printed in Great Britain by The Bath Press

PART ONE

THE PHOTOGRAPHER

CHAPTER I

My point is that I know the story so well now that I almost fear for the telephone to ring in my own house once darkness has fallen. A phone call late at night always causes unease, even in the most ordered household, it is an intrusion, a call from beyond the safety of the hearth. And when it comes a little before dawn, or a little before 3 a.m. in a strange and isolated house, as it did for my dearest, for my closest friend Joe, then that strangeness must be dreadfully increased.

He was dead asleep after the day's long journey, not even aware the rented cottage possessed a telephone. At least the moon was full and there was light on the stairs for him, and even glimmers down the hall into what had once been the front room. Each stumbled step he expected the caller to ring off but the bell was ceaseless, loud, insistent, echoing around the long-empty house. He found the telephone after a good minute's search. It was of a long-disused design and for more seconds he fumbled, clumsy with its unfamiliarity before finding the receiver. 'Hello,' he said. 'Hello.' There was no reply. 'Hello, Joe here,' he repeated once more. Still there was silence. The line, he was sure, was not dead but rather someone hung on, silent to his greeting. Of course he was chilled by it all. He tried again. 'Hello, this is Joe. I am the new resident here in Mossymere and . . .' The receiver now clicked. The line started to buzz.

Puzzled, Joe returned to the bedroom where the moon flooded through the curtainless windows. His heart still beat rapidly as it does when a man is so shaken out of a deep sleep, but slowly it calmed and into the quiet night he sank once more. Minutes past 3 o'clock, the telephone rang a second time. It rang until he was awake. It rang all the time he decided to ignore it and it was still ringing to the moment he gave in and crossed the room towards it the second time. He grasped the receiver, put it to his ear, but even before he could say a word, the caller had clicked off. All he had heard was what sounded like the rushing of a gale, like the whistle of a high and rising wind. There had not been a word. He stood in a pool of moonbeam, quite naked, holding a dead telephone. The first call had been an irritation but this one following had unsettled Joe badly. It surely was calculated, was born out of some deep and frightening emotion. The act was the expression of malice perhaps, and deliberately designed to alarm. At that time the possibility did not occur to Joe of the caller's sad desire for contact, a pathetic yearning for something that cannot be.

There was no electricity in the house and Joe had not had time to prime any lamps, yet the short June night was wearing thin and in the quickening grey of the dawn he looked at the telephone. It could well be half a century old, he thought, and now it was layered thick in dust and cobweb. Well it might have been, for no one had lived in Mossymere for years. Joe fingered the instrument over and over. In his hands now, close to sun rise, there was not even a dialling tone. It was black, it was dead and it was useless and he could not understand the calls of the night. He had been in the house barely three or four hours. It was dark on his arrival and no more than three people knew of his stay alone in the cottage in the great wood. He wondered if he were being watched, but even as he thought it, he knew he was being absurd. There was not a house for close on a mile and that had lain unoccupied even longer than Mossymere – ever since its own particular tragedy of near sixty years before. The village was still further away and completely curtained off by the thick acres of the oak wood.

Despite the moon and the clarity of the skies, the night, the dawn even, was warm and Joe sat on the pantiles as his flesh turned from ivory to grey to brown. Outside a pheasant called from a long-uncut hedgerow. Upstairs, sparrows had wakened to rustle in the straws beneath the pantiles and soon they were singing in the new day's light. Night, only two hours back in time, was a dust.

Chapter II

Joe went out to his car, parked in a clearing of the trees, pushed into the bracken. From the boot he brought two camera cases into the house. That first morning back in Mossymere, he was eager to work and the dawn offered him special opportunities of light and mist and even the chance of deer by the river or a fox coming in home with a meal of young rabbit in his jaws. Loaded with films and lenses, he stepped outside the doorway and made his path through the long grass so wet with dew. The world smelled fresh to him and clean and a jay flickered away, crying anger, calling alarm. His dark tracks through the silver began to meander. He began to dance. This was joy.

This was the Mossymere that he had known. It was for days and dusks and dawns such as these that Joe had chosen to return after so many years. As soon as I had confirmed the commission, as soon as contracts had been signed, he knew there was only one place to spend his summer. He told me if he were to make a success of the work in hand he would have to realise a dream that he had always held on to. He would have to portray the world of Mossymere as it had existed, breathed and grown in his mind, in his memory for some twenty years. Then and sometimes since, he had talked to me of this far off land and nothing else would do but the images of that time-lost place he had known as a student. I have no doubt that to Joe, the estate, the domain, call it what we will, seemed to be a life as it had been forever – long long ago, before time and progress caught up with the world outside and scarred it indelibly. As a young man, he had not been able to see any divide between past and present there and through the years that he was away from Mossymere they intermingled to become a corner lost somewhere in time that he always yearned to return to. He had left his heart in that place, though now I know why he took so long to make his way back there in full maturity.

He felt that if only he could live again in that great wood then his work would be secure. There was one house in particular that he told me he just had to rent. It meant something to him that I only half realised then but he did say how he first found it. He was very vague over the month, the year even, and yet he could recall the day with absolute clarity.

The night had been stormy and though the strong winds had dropped, both the dawn and the morning were soakingly wet with continual presence of thunder. The potato field on which he had been working ran awash. The headlands even were sodden. The furrows ran with streams strong enough to carry gravel and silt into the lowes where the toads lay buried and the crop was beaten. The farmhouse had been flooded from its swollen pond. Bullocks had paddled into the yard when he arrived and Joe's instructions for the day, understandably as a student there, came last. He was to look for an axe that the woodman had left somewhere in the Mossymere forest, buried hilt deep in one of the million trees that streamed the warm summer rain.

He followed a finger pointed vaguely towards a likely drive through the woodland and he entered into a haze of green mists and spirals of smoke and mosquitoes that swarmed the damp air and the rain that still fell. And fell from the bracken and the oaks and ashes and the long untrodden grass. He entered a hut when the rain became particularly intense. Standing by the door he watched skeletons of stoats and weasels wind-dance on a derelict keeper's line. The door itself was hacked with hearts and initials and short messages. Once, obviously long long before, the shed had been a haven – dark, deserted, used for love.

Away Joe went again on his fool's errand, down the endless overgrown rides. Path gave into path and the wood closed in deeper and wilder as he walked. Only the sighing of rain. Just the washing of tears through the green curtains where an owl called by day. No sun. No shadows. No direction and no axe. He came upon a new plantation and followed it down to a stile. He paused there but the flies that had tailed him through the forest caught him now in a fury around his head. Waving them away, he slipped on the mossed planking and tumbled his length into the bracken. Close by, a dog barked and Joe followed the sound.

In a clearing, he had stumbled across the house in Mossymere. Black dog guarding the gate, geese that came at him as he went up to ask his way. An ageing man called him in, to come along out of the wet there, and in a dark kitchen he stood. Cats were asleep on a floor of potato sacking. The dog inspected the stranger, hackles still high, growls still deep and low in the barrel chest.

'Looking for an axe. Blast me, it's not like Ian to waste a man's time on damn nonsense. He could have sent you away to dinner and done no harm by it. I don't doubt all this will clear by the afternoon.'

'It will be too wet still for the machine though,' Joe replied. 'The potato field's like a pudding all over and we'd sink within a yard.'

'The potato machine?' The old man looked attentively at Joe. 'You'll be the student my wife knows then. I've heard a fair bit of you since she's worked the riddle this month.'

Suddenly the man lost his facelessness. You are Maggie's

husband, Joe thought. You. You, a grey stooping man alone in this dark, dripping kingdom.

The dog now began to growl openly and show its teeth and, following further directions, Joe left to make his way back to the farmyard as best he could. He turned around after only a half-minute's walk and already the house was lost again in the forest and only a curl of wood smoke above the oak tops offered a clue to its existence.

CHAPTER III

I have always believed Joe to be wildly fantastical and indeed the hallmark of his work has been his ability to convey impressions, desires and dreams on film, something that I myself have never been able to do. I also know how great the impact the Mossymere house had on him; so immense that at one time he had set out to find everything about its past.

He told me once that it was built on the site of an ancient ruin and for centuries few people had ever visited there, on a path to nowhere but the Devil's Dish, once a flint mine and for 2,000 years or more, a lonesome and benighted place. Only tramps and poor travellers stopped over there in the depths of winter, sheltering under a scrap of roof, or in the lee of a half-standing wall. There they passed the short days, the endless nights, haggard with cold and hunger. So it always had been at this place where people came, a pace before death, drifting on the wind, castaways in life.

The age of the dwelling, its first purpose and why it came to be abandoned, Joe could not discover, but there dawned a day early this century when work began on the ruined walls. Materials were carted a mile down the track into the wood and then barrowed deeper in still when the path dwindled out. Bricks, tiles and timber were collected and the labourers were drawn from all over the estate for the reconstruction. What was sound was left and a new body was implanted upon the ancient shell. Hacked clear of plaster remnants the walls told their own tale. A skeleton of medieval bricks held in the guts of the building, nothing but simple rubble collected from the woodland clearings. Flints had taken the place of bricks, laid in crazy patterns, many had once been fashioned into hand axes, scrapers and even daggers. There were slabs of tile salvaged from a Roman villa that were all blackened from the fires of darkness and chaos. There were bones in the wall too, of men it was said, as well as of wolf, deer and dog. There were lumps of stone, crudely painted and carved and there were fossils, left from the retreat of the ice-cap when the estate was born under storms and leaden skies. Red pamment tiles were placed upon the sand floors, the wide fireplace of old was narrowed and a small stove was fitted in, with a towering chimney stack, pot topped, to snatch all the breeze it could from the grip of the surrounding forest. A well was dug. Windows, doors, a fence even was run around and the work was finished by high summer when the men were removed to prepare for the harvest. What was not done would have to be completed by the incomer.

The site had been well chosen for a keeper's cottage, there in the heart of Mossymere, near to the sand hills known as Foxburrows. Foxes had dominated there ever since the landscape matured, once the blue ice sheets had begun to succumb to warmer summers and when the melt waters had started to flow in milk white torrents down innumerable valleys, leaving sand and gravel deposits in their wake. Some centuries of renewed cold and ice reformed and the estate lay like the arctic tundras of today when strange birds wheel in empty skies and carry from the south the seeds of future forests in their crops.

At last, in warmer centuries still, broad-leaved woodland of oak, lime and elm spread over the light soils. The scrub filled out dense and bracken spread until even in broad daylight only flickers of light reached the peat-covered ground. To this place the foxes had come, to the dry slopes that faced the warm south. Their earths were countless centuries old. The whole woodland there was tunnelled and re-tunnelled, an endless maze of warrens that tied together like a knot beneath this the foxes' bastion. The very soil that ran between a man's fingers there had come to smell of fox and their prey. The scent of musk lay over the earths as tangible as a mist over a lake at dawn. Foxburrows was a stronghold, a castle, a keep, and from it for nights of thousands of years the hunters had poured to loot the surrounding land. They had plundered the wild pheasants and partridges, the voles, the mice, the rats and the shrews and when the village appeared, chickens from the little back yards. They raided the isolated farms to steal the eggs from beneath the geese, the scraps from the rubbish tips and to be back in the tanglewood before dawn.

The completed house stood empty a month. The forest began to creep back on it when, come a high summer evening, the keeper arrived. The still air smelled of harvest, the sun slanted low over the Mossymere treetops and the dust from his cart hung in a golden cloud behind him. His young wife lay asleep. The horse was tired, his head drooped low and the dogs trailed a long way behind, one a little lame. The family had come from afar, had slept one night on the road, another in a hayloft and now there was no one in Mossymere to greet them, just the bare house, its damp plaster, its walled-up bones and past. The cart had to be left away from the house and the young people walked up the slightly rising ground that was the fringe of Foxburrows. Like galaxies of stars in the night, pale eyes glittered at their coming. The whole ground tremored to their step as if exposed nerves were being trodden on. The stove was lit and for the first time in hundreds of years, smoke whispered through the chimney. The dogs barked and all night the girl-wife looked out through the bare dark windows that threw her slim tear-streaked beauty back into the room where the keeper lay collapsed on the pillows unconscious to the vixen's barking of the primeval songs of the forest.

It was to this house that Joe, at the break point between youth and middle age, had been so desperate to return.

CHAPTER IV

I do know that almost immediately after his arrival, Joe investigated a barn, now derelict, that stands close to the Mossymere house. The evening before, perhaps his first, he had watched a white owl quartering the water meadow and the wood fringe and he had guessed at its roost. The crumbled red brick rampart at the head of the valley was ideal for the bird and there it was betrayed by its cascade of droppings down lime-cemented walls. Its nest was a chink between dusted straw bales and was watched by Joe for a good while as he brooded on a photographic assault. And, yes, it's true, he let his mind run back those years to when the barn was a paradise for him. There was not much he had forgotten, for Joe was never careless with magic; not the view over the valley and Mossymere; not the wormed step-ladder to the hayloft and not the arrow-slit chink of window to the south where he once lay to watch the track to the weather-blasted door. The naturalist in him now. That opening, so close to the owl's roost would surely be the snow bird's exit. And so it proved as the shadows fell on Joe's second Mossymere day and the soundless wings, framed a second in ancient flint, mothed away over the corn.

A hide on the crest of the bullock yard wall would be on beak level with the owl's gateway and only ten yards away and so it was there that Joe began work the very next morning, a little after the sunrise. He worked very hard and quietly – the estate had taught him to do that as a mere boy – to finish long before late afternoon when the bird might even suspect the coming of dusk and begin to stir. Very occasionally during the day, Joe slipped inside the barn to check on the bird's presence. Joe is like that; he cannot let a good thing be; he could not, I suspect, let his memories rest; but the glint of beak remained unmoved the day through as if hewed from ivory. The job was finished. Satisfied, Joe climbed into the canvas a last time to check on the angles, the distance and the overall stability of his construction. He was well pleased as the June sun began at last to falter and frame him up high in admiration of the whole scene.

Across the hedgerows to the Mossymere house, the rabbits were already appearing as unmolested creatures of brown, now that the estate was without a keeper. The sun by now was low enough to catch on the windows of his new house and they blazed back at him like shields. He was understandably moved to take a photograph. With a long lens he focused on the brickwork, the patterns of the pantiles, even picking out the telephone wire – the telephone wire from the house that he followed all the way to a bracket on the side of the barn. There it was snapped. Cut. Whatever, but for sure it was ended there and did not continue to the telegraph post a hundred yards distant. Joe put down the camera. His immediate impulse was to climb the jagged brickwork to inspect the shorn cable and to determine how long the Mossymere telephone had been disconnected. To do that, though, would alarm the owl and that, too, would be giving way to the disquiet growing within him. He had seen no one round the house since his arrival to have tampered with the telephone that rang so clearly his first night. And why take a telephone off now when after years the house was once more tenanted?

That moment, Joe's most wonderful landscape was tainted for him and even the silence, once so blessed, seemed somehow now sinister. Sad that a man in his paradise refound should be aware of reaching shadows and look in something like fear at the darkening wood around him.

He walked slowly down the meadow, back into the house without hesitation to the telephone on the window seat. He examined his fingerprints on the receiver and the disturbed dust on the sill where he had scraped the instrument in confusion that first night. Again he lifted the aged batten-like receiver and listened. The line was quite dead. It ended at the owl's barn. That, Joe knew, was a torment over. Any further intrusion would be unthinkable and the knowledge of it made him happier. Then, the absurdity of it all made him smile and he went outside once more to enjoy the last of the evening light.

My guess is that he wallowed in the idea of his seclusion. His escape from a world he found increasingly sterile must have seemed near complete. Perhaps he worried about a few weekend visits to the city, to the family, to his studio. Perhaps he felt some anxiety over the work he had to do, but I doubt it. I suspect he went to bed as clear in his mind as he had been for years, probably since he last knew Mossymere even. The glory of his youth, when all was happiness and light and satisfaction, he half imagined to be preparing to rise from the ashes of his dawning middle age. And I knew he felt himself to be sufficiently agile to catch the phoenix, should the bird ever look like escape.

CHAPTER V

Joe was startled to be awakened by a postman and, not having delivered a letter to Mossymere for nearly nineteen years, the postman himself must have felt some curiosity. It was a delivery of importance: an invitation to the hall for a drinks party and so it was Joe pulled the door behind him at 7 o'clock that same evening and stepped off into the wood. He sensed himself bizarrely overdressed for a walk of a mile or more over track and meadow but he refused to drive so short a way. If his white shoes scuffed, his cream trousers stained from the bracken or his dazzling shirt caught in any brambles, the smart company at Swancoots would have to accept it. Joe was not in Mossymere to make concessions to anyone. Quite why he had been invited to such an occasion by Nicholas, he did not know, but he had his suspicions. His photographs had been published world-over and he knew he was a minor celebrity. Nicholas would like that. And the fact that Joe had once worked on the estate Nicholas would find amusing. Nicholas had always been one to revel in any glory, never mind if they were only reflections. And ricocheted at that.

Joe would be proved right on all points as the evening lengthened. The sun was still high on the dusty summer track. The cow parsley was tall and the rabbits were playing, so many, so soon, without any fear. Since the keeper had left Mossymere, they had multiplied to become a plague and though the foxes had returned too in numbers, they could not make serious inroads. After a half-mile Joe turned into a field and followed a headland towards the nearing towers. As he skirted the corn he pulled instinctively at the wild oats, his old job in days of rain when the potato harvester would sink. Never then had he seen the weeds grow in such profusion, like a film now over the crop beneath. But then the hedgerow itself was wild and unkempt and the brambles and ivory smothered the saplings that had been planted twenty years back in Joe's summer there. And yet, there could be no denial of the beauty of the estate. Neglect had even enhanced its features, as though everything was seen in soft focus now with the sharp edges, the farmed preciseness, all removed. Everything could still glow golden on such a June night and if nature were nibbling back here and there, Joe could not see that as a bad thing in the over-manicured world he so hated.

Through the gates and on the roadway through the small park, Joe could look around with genuine wonderment. Never, though he had once queued at the hall every week to receive his wages, had he seen these grounds look so fabulous. The ancient brickwork, the mullioned windows, the towers burned like steeples in the sun. The family flag flew proud and reflected on a moat, still, clear, and boated with gaily decked lilies. White willows draped the lake. Strange plants cast perfumes as strong as woodman's smoke into his eyes and his nostrils. Lawns were as green and as rolled as billiard baize. Lavender bloomed like Alpine skies and shook Medusa locks of evening bees. Copper-shielded beeches and oaks proud since the armada whispered beauty everywhere. The hall existed from another time and from another place and in those bars of sunlight held Joe in thrall.

His pace had slowed down to nothing. He was at sea in the ocean of the exotic, the sensual and the sublime.

Nicholas was watching, delighted, from the moat drawbridge. He came forward to greet his last guest.

'Joe,' Nicholas said. 'It's good to see you again after such a long time. How long must it be then?'

'Twenty years exactly.'

'God, that long. I was trying to work it out myself but didn't reckon on that. Of course, now I come to think of it, I could have judged from that other party you attended.'

Joe laughed, 'I am surprised you brought that affair up.'

'Why not?' Nicholas asked. 'I don't remember it as going too badly.'

'Our memories of it differ then,' Joe replied.

'Well - it was a long time ago and whose memory is infallible after all?'

Joe simply shrugged his shoulders and Nicholas led the way into the rose garden where the party had assembled.

There the barrage of colour was even greater, as if every shade, every shot, every dream ever dreamed of and then cunningly created had been splashed over the full blooms and flowing dresses of the ladies. Joe was introduced as the famous wildlife photographer, which he politely disclaimed, and as the man who had worked on the estate in his youth, which he quietly accepted as a deeper truth than any there would ever guess. There were many there who wanted to speak to him, as one well known and as a newcomer to a small and close society where any fresh mind is seen as inspiration or escapism.

It was with Anne that he remained when the pollen around him had settled. She was an elderly lady, not true village, but having bought on retirement the house once a schoolroom in days past.

'I was an art mistress all my working life,' she told Joe. 'So when I say I admire your work I like to think that I am one who knows. It was your last book that really intrigued me. I'll be honest.' She paused. 'I think it was loads better than the first. There was more of a concept there. More of a plan. You seem to have a tale to tell and it hung together so much more tightly somehow. There was a beauty of idea there – not just form. Something I had never really considered in photography before.'

'Miss Walker.'

'Do call me Anne.'

'Anne, then, it was just simpler that second book. What I portrayed was river, no more, no less than what it was and what it suffered. I didn't make it. I didn't change it or direct it or influence it in any way. All I did was photograph it using all the tricks of a profession I am skilled in. Half the shots were faked and you are now near applauding them as art. Which they are not.'

'But they are beautiful, that's the point. It's the end result of anything that matters and you achieve perfection many, many times. There was a heron shot, you know, that will never be done better.'

'Not until somebody thinks up a better trick. That's why I'm here. There are schemes that stand by themselves without the need to fake. If you like, I see some honest beauty here I've always wanted to portray. Mossymere won't need gimmicks or touch-ups – not even filters half the time. It's the light that is so special, so unique. It is all around you some days and it can make anything alive and vibrant.'

'My God, Joe,' Anne smiled, 'you are suffering a teenage crush on the place. Rose tinted lenses of your youth I suggest! Did you lose your heart here? Probably what you thought beautiful then didn't really exist and it certainly doesn't now. Beware of returning where the memory is sweet. You can't call these gardens for instance anything but a riot of bad taste.' Joe said nothing.

'I'd expect you to agree with me at once somehow,' she continued. 'Can't you see how ludicrous a place it is with that, that jester in control here.' She pointed at Nicholas sipping a goblet of white wine wearing rose petals floating like pink clouds. 'That skunk basking there in his own self esteem. You know, don't you, the entire estate is collapsing around him. Have you any idea what the cottages are like? Your beloved Mossymere house is a dream in June but imagine what it is like in winter. Some snow and rain through the roof would bring you up sharp enough. Especially if you had to live on the wages he pays.'

'If it's such a cheerless place, why did you come here? Why do you stay?'

'Perhaps, Joe, I thought like you but I am just seeing the truth. About him – Nicholas – the estate, the village, the gossip, everything.' Her anger was real. She put down her glass and lifted away a hand quite shaking with rage. She calmed, smiled and said, 'Once that would have been my definition of beauty.'

Joe followed her nod towards a girl just come into the garden and standing quietly in a fountain of damask rose. She was tall, slim and dark headed. Her skin looked very bronzed, but that could have been a trick of the descending dusk. She stood alone, her eyes pools of shadow, perhaps looking at him, Joe thought, or more simply into the night on errands of her own. She was young, in her teens or early twenties at most, but a deep red, clinging dress lent an air of sophistication, of knowledge to her.

'The look on your face suggests you'd agree with me,' Anne said as the girl moved away further under the trees. When she had quite faded from Joe's sight, he asked her name.

'Swallow.'

'Swallow – like the bird?'

'Yes, as you say. Why I'm not sure, but the story goes,' she whispered, teeth white in the gloom, 'that she was conceived in the late summer and her mother chose the name of the migratory swallow just after the birth and just before she herself died.'

'Her father?'

Anne shrugged. 'She lives with him – an old man – down in the village. He is well into his seventies. No, probably eighties actually. There is a rumour Swallow is not his, but I don't think anyone knows. The age gap is probably the only basis for that I should think. Though I don't believe they are particularly close. They live together, but little else, I'm told.'

'What does she do here?'

'Do! Does anyone looking like her need to do anything? If I would pay to look at her, I'm sure men would do as much! She's Nicholas's ultimate ornament. You know he really is a skunk. She pretends to help here and there on the estate, exercising the horses mostly. But she's cosmetic really. Not a bad life, except that Nicholas is the price she pays.' Joe raised his eyebrows.

'Well, my dear, I don't know for sure but so says village gossip.'

'Don't you go too much on that, Anne.'

'Only when I like what it says then I do.'

The night grew even more beautiful, the colours deeper and the trees quieter as the last breezes settled over the sleeping countryside. By ten, there was complete quiet but for the guests talking in the afterglow. Bats flickered in and out of the bell tower and someone remarked that the midges were terrible in the still, almost sultry air. Nicholas, though, made no move to open the hall and in groups, people pardoned themselves and faded away into the night. Joe and Anne were the last to leave and Joe accompanied her to the drive before making his own way back to Mossymere. He was in no hurry. He stopped on a hedgerow to listen. He relived the garden party and listened to Anne over in his mind.

'Lost his heart in Mossymere', she had said. Twenty years ago. That other party. He tried hard to think about it, but his memory was faded on the details. Even *her* face was no longer clear to him, not after so long a time and God knows how many times he had tried to recapture it, breathe it to life. Perhaps if he were a painter, not a photographer, he could have achieved the resurrection, but as he knew, he was no artist, no creator. He wondered why he had not mentioned her to Nicholas: he had the chance. Apprehension, he supposed it was – or the fear that had always prevented him making any contact after that last night in Mossymere.

He had taken an hour over the quarter-mile to his track into the wood when he heard an engine back at the hall. The car came his way, Nicholas's, and as he pressed himself back into the cow parsley it passed him. Swallow was in the passenger seat. For a second, Joe saw her finely-cut profile against the bright western sky. For another second, he swore she had turned to look at him as they passed by.

CHAPTER VI

Joe slept the following morning and was awakened by the postman's call. I had sent a registered letter, returning some prints for him to sign for.

'Lovely day, again,' the postman had said. Joe was still tired and rather abrupt.

'Yes.'

'You've missed the best of it I'd say,' the postman went on.

'Actually I was up until dawn. I had some photography on and I have only been in bed a couple of hours.'

'So then you're not pleased I've called, I'll bet.'

Joe softened, 'Don't worry. I'm well awake now. Come in for a coffee. I'm having one.' The postman hardly hesitated. Joe was an object of interest in the estate and it was good to have the gossip.

He returned to his van, stopped the engine and came back to the kitchen. The two men sat over a pot of coffee and a plate of far from fresh cake. Joe, though, always had the ability to charm and I suspect the postman soon felt at ease, an important person even, the centre of vital events. Joe knew him from his student summer.

'You've been on this round a long time, haven't you?' he asked.

'I'll say. Twenty-seven years and I've seen a few changes take place! First I walked, then I biked and now I've got my van. That's a blessing. Winter specially. You couldn't guess what it was like then in the old days.'

'Have the people changed much?'

'Less of them, that's all. Same families, but fewer kids. Fewer jobs on the estate too, so many have had to leave. See how many of the cottages are left to fall in. There are days I hardly have to deliver a single letter to the village. Apart from Swancoots, that is.'

'So you'd remember the people here before me? An older man with a much younger wife.' Joe held his breath.

'The Lengthsman, and Maggie?'

'Yes. Yes. Where are they?'

'He's in the village. She died.'

Joe stood up at once. The postman followed him rather alarmed.

'Sorry,' said Joe. 'Thought I heard a rat again under the sink somewhere.'

The two men rummaged there a while, fruitlessly.

'Funny old things, rats,' said the postman. 'I'll bet they're everywhere under these tiles. They make runs in the sand beneath and they're the devil to get out, once they're there.' He promised to call with some traps and Joe went with him to the van.

He did not look at the photographs, he told me. He returned to bed, not so much to sleep, but rather to huddle there and to cry inwardly at what the postman had so sadly told him.

CHAPTER VII

In his first weeks or perhaps after a month or so at Mossymere, I went to visit Joe, primarily to discuss his work and to see how the book was developing but also out of curiosity. I wanted to see, I suppose, if Joe had captured the dream, one so strong that even I as a friend was touched by it. Certainly, I found him changed in some subtle ways that I noticed, but could not describe later easily, when asked.

Personally, I was not happy in the Mossymere house. It had been long deserted and smelled of must and damp. The bare walls, the stained ceilings, the grimed window panes all depressed me and I found the forest gloomy too, dark and claustrophobic outside.

From the start, I found myself tense and quite irritable there. I doubted if Joe were eating well – though there was plenty of evidence of heavy drinking, both from the bottles around and from his own pallid complexion. I was also disappointed by the lack of progress with his book. He had been some while in Mossymere and I really could see little evidence of that in terms of output. Joe, though, was insistent that ideas were taking shape.

What alarmed me most as publisher, was that he was now talking about centering the book around a girl.

'But, Joe, the commission is to record a modern-day wood. It's simply natural history. I cannot for the life of me see where she would fit in.'

'Then I'll change the book,' was all Joe replied and I knew from very long experience of him that further argument then, there, would be useless.

Her name, of course, was Swallow but what so attracted Joe he found hard to define for me. After all, he had photographed the most beautiful women the world over and the allure of looks alone he knew well enough. Lovely no doubt he found Swallow, but there was more, much more, that he saw in her. Or thought, or dreamed that he did in that lonely place.

He said her lack of affectation attracted him – the way she ran here and there like a little girl still and cared nothing for the rain which drenched her clothing down tight over a slender almost immature figure. He liked to see lengths of straws abandoned in her hair and the utterly forgotten tears in her clothing that showed her legs as brown as her arms or her face. She had a tan like a fawn's as though she had been veneered by the elements of nature. He told me that he knew well enough that this itself could all be a trick, a pose just as calculated as any other man or woman dreams up to suit. Yet her eyes he said denied all guile.

'Not her eyes. Not her damned, deep brown eyes. They well back somehow and back, endlessly – like oceans of innocence,' I think he said. I believe that day that he was drowning in them. He told me the art teacher's explanation of her name.

'The summer girl. Brown as a nut ripening on a tree. A summer swallow, swooping, soaring.' And I knew his heart and his soul were with her every wing beat.

He said he knew how juvenile all this was – at the beginning. At the beginning, he could put this adolescence in him away for most of, no all, the day, and only bring it out in the evening, or when he wished, as a kind of toy to play with, to amuse him. That was when the feeling was tamed, controllable, something he could pick up and put down at will.

Through her name he conceived the desire to photograph swallows at sunset. He had spent a great deal of time on the shot, trying for nostalgia, for a summer that would come to its end. I looked at the prints, which were good in their way: all golden glows whispering harvest and farewells to a happy life. I knew that the swallows were important in themselves as winged reminders to Joe of change and movement and of the freedom that he had been yearning for.

The girl, for that very reason he felt, must have been named by fate. Obviously he had spent a great deal of time on these prints choosing exactly the beat of river where a cornfield dipped to meet it and where the sun could be framed against the stand of oak as it set. He explained how the shape of the trees themselves attracted him. In their venerable way, they represented a promise of future summers, of sunset swallows sipping of the stream. Eternity. The whole concept pleased him greatly and when at last he squeezed the shutter on the thirtieth of a second, he had felt something special was locked away.

This I do believe was all Swallow herself was to him at that fateful beginning. She was an ornament.

'And then,' said Joe, 'she touched me, which in itself was strange for two people who had never spoken.'

He was by the water mill. He had been there for several hours, hidden up behind some willow herb with a fishing rod put over the white water, hoping for a kingfisher to alight long enough for a few frames. Several times the emerald bird had hovered, but in the end it always veered off, piping alarm. Each occasion, Joe's finger had relaxed from the shutter and his wait had continued. He was more patient than any normal angler. He would have shamed the most imperturbable heron. He was not concerned, time was on his side. The day was warm, the rose-bays smelled sweet and threw him back constantly to a childhood memory he sought hard to find. There was a great deal for him to feel glad about.

Sometime before lunch, he heard the ring of hooves on the lane behind him. He dare not look round for fear of alarming the bird, let alone move, but when the animal began to splash heavily at the tail of the weir and the little blue bird sped away upstream and round a bend in the river, then he was angry. He sprang up and burst through the reeds on to the grassy riverbank. He was greeted there by a girl's laughter.

Swallow was wading the river with her horse. Her jeans were sodden. Her shirt clung to her. Her hair hung in brown rat's tails and her hazel eyes were on him. She saw his hide and his anger as clearly as she had seen the kingfisher depart. She waded from the river laughing still and placed her cool hand gently on his forearm.

'God,' she said, 'I am so sorry. I should think you're cursing me and the mare aren't you?' All the while she spoke she had left her fingers brushing him and that simple physical pressure had ripped the veil of imagination that Joe had put up between them. No longer could she be a fairy, or a photograph. Now Swallow, this live lovely girl, had swooped right under his ribs and into his heart.

Joe told me how he had struggled for words, as if the few droplets of water Swallow put on him were torrents of ice-cold mountain streams. Still she continued to stroke his hairs with her fingertips and her eyes held his and though the whole affair lasted only seconds, Joe felt his whole life was run. It was as though he had been bodily crushed, as though she had drawn something from him that could never be replaced.

'No, no,' he had stammered. 'It doesn't matter. You were hardly to know, were you? After all I was not meant to be advertising my presence exactly! No. The fault was nearly all mine.' Swallow smiled. Her lips glistened, wet. Her teeth glittered.

'Well, how about me?' she had asked.

'You?'

'Yes. Why not photograph me and the mare? Call it "Cow Girl In The Sand", or "Two Old Cows At The Mill". Even better, as I am sure that's what you're still thinking!'

But then he did not photograph her. She had not really meant what she said and swung up on to the mare once more and moved her way down the lane again. She had gone ten yards when she turned round and called.

'Good luck. I'll come back a different way. Promise!' She waved. Her thrush-egg arm caught the sun and she was hidden by a dogleg in the track.

The kingfisher did not return. In the late June afternoon a few mayfly hatched out of the chalk stream to celebrate their brief life and he photographed them in their spirals and glitters of dusts of gold. Trout began to plop. A swallow dropped from the mill eaves and then the hatch was done. I asked Joe how he felt and all he replied was that he had taken a long way home to Mossymere, along the river course where the watercress grew rank and where the hay was ready for cutting. It was hardly the trout stream he had known his first summer on the estate, he said. The gravels had silted and the groynes and fish weirs were all tumbledown since the river keeper had retired and had not been replaced. Flashes of chalk could be seen to gleam in places as a memory of what the little river once had been and he felt he must speak to Nicholas, to do something before he left at the end of the summer.

Chapter VIII

His path from the river that night took him through the village at last. A few children stood on the bridge, fishing, idling, watching him as he walked through them. Along the old street odd doors were open to catch the last of the sun before it sank behind the poplars and the pantiles. In the patch of allotments there were gardeners and the faces of good old boys that he knew he recognised from long ago. Some wished him good evening and others merely watched. But by all his presence in their midst was noted.

He stopped at the village telephone kiosk. The city number rang several times before it was answered - she would be outside with the children.

'Jan, darling, Joe here.'

'Hello darling, thank you, thank you for phoning. I can't tell you how we're looking forward to the weekend - Ben was just talking about you and I was saying . . .'

Joe cut in 'Jan, that's why I'm calling.' In the long silence, he continued. 'You see, baby, I'm getting somewhere with a barn owl at last. The hide has been up a good while and he's well and truly used to it. What I really want is a big full moon and I'll get that Saturday or Sunday. The weather looks good, the skies should be clear and so things will never be better. I'd be tempted to leave him for the next full one, but the harvest will be on then and heaven knows how the bird will react. The odds are he'll be off and I'd have missed him altogether.' Still there was no city reply. He tried again. 'Jan, honestly, I'd rather be coming home to you and the children. I'm desperately lonely and I'm missing you all like hell. Believe me, I don't like this any more than you do.'

A quiet voice. 'Honestly?' it asked.

'Honestly,' he lied. He had finished the barn owl days before – he had wanted a crescent moon for the shot never a full one. And the farmer had already cleared out the barn for harvest time. The white owl was long gone.

'I'm sorry,' Jan said again. 'Just so long as you love me still. Sometimes I do feel insecure and lonely too. But I know you'd come if you could. Any chance of next weekend instead?'

'That's a definite yes,' Joe replied. They rang off and the hundreds of miles flooded in again between them. She walked away into a lonely suburban evening. He felt unburdened again, free in the country, and he did not hurry back to Mossymere.

Rather he stopped at the local inn, The Nelson, where the room was as he had remembered it, down to the tiled floor, the small serving hatch that was used as a bar and the walls bare of useless ornament or affectation. It was an estate man's pub that he had once loved for its directness of purpose: strangers were little encouraged and certainly there were none of the more exotic drinks that the wandering visitor might ask for. The landlady could roll her forbidding eyes and tell them straight, 'That's not on. No we don't have that neither. That's off an' all. Well, there's beer and there's gin. And some whisky if you're quick about it. No, we don't do food. No call for it. Everyone's got homes to go to here.'

Few people that were fresh to The Nelson stayed there long and even Joe felt inhibited as he crossed the threshold after some two decades. He was not recognised by the half dozen men, playing crib, smoking or talking slowly of the harvest, but Joe, however, knew them nearly all.

To them the place was a nest, a place of security and warmth. The landlady was order and purpose, the mother they had known and probably lost decades before. For a while he was disturbed how little they had changed and how far he was removed from the lad he once had been. Life he felt had scathed him as it had not these one time workmates. Perhaps he was bitter; more like self indulgent which soon faded when he recognised the one man whose name escaped him. With a deep shock he realised the ageing man, apart from the rest, was Ian, the farm manager of his day. Now he looked grey, tired, shabby around the corners somehow and not at all the fine man of the past.

Even to see Ian in the pub troubled Joe and when the big man brushed past him to the counter for a whisky, a large one, he was even further disturbed.

'That's your last, Ian,' the landlady said. 'You'll not be finding your way home again if we're not careful with you.' The room fell to a hush. A dice fell to its side. A gang of flat-capped heads turned Ian's way.

'Not to be a bother to anyone, I'll be on my way now then,' he said heavily and pushed towards the door.

'Poor bugger,' a man said as the latch clicked behind him.

'We'd all second that,' another replied and then after its brief pause life went on as before.

Joe went quickly outside and looked up and down the lane: he ran to the bend and then the other way over the bridge, but in so short a time, Ian had disappeared into the late evening.

Puzzled, depressed, he returned to the bar but received little information there.

'One too many an argument with Nicholas and got his cards. He'd rowed with old Lordie and got away with it, but not Nicholas, who'll take umbrage at not a lot at all. Then there was his wife and then, then – oh lots of things and so he is like he is now. Do you know him then?' the landlady asked.

'I did,' said Joe. 'I found him a very good man.'

One of the old boys, Lennie, if Joe remembered right, looked at him queerly and Joe drank up and left before he too should be questioned. He did not need his own life to be exposed in any way at all.

CHAPTER IX

I shifted in my chair. I find it hard to express the discomfort I felt at Joe's tale. Sadness, lies, guilt and decay – I could not see at all why he stayed on in this place. The sun that had greeted my visit had moved away and the room was quite dark enough for a lamp, though I suspect it was not even midday. Joe had been drinking all through his story and now the whole room smelled quite strongly of alcohol. I suggested a walk. He would have nothing of that but told me he desperately wanted to continue with the events of that particular evening.

He left the inn when the lights were needed about 9 o'clock in July, a night or so before the full moon. He went out into the village street as the first bats flickered from the roof spaces and the barns. He crossed the river where the geese were penned and walked to the deserted blacksmith's house on the fringes of Mossymere.

He stood outside it a long while, thinking that from it a person could perhaps see the Mossymere house. From the very first, ever since the telephone's ring, he had felt himself watched in some way. I broke in and interrupted him to say that it was the nature of the house itself, the closeness of the forest, but I saw that he had not even listened to me at all.

And so now he checked the dirt outside the gate of Robert's farmhouse, as it was called. Not only were there no footprints, but the gate had jammed so hard that Joe needed to strain to move it. The garden was overgrown. Untrodden nettle and bramble grew in tangles up to the doors. Guttering hung down and tiles were off. Several windows were broken and the back door swung open as Joe pushed it. He entered a dark corridor. It was foul, running with damp. A den of rats, lair of foxes, it had been shunned by man for decades and Joe wandered from room to broken room.

The kitchen was ruined. The dairy wall was badly bowed in. In the drawing-room a soot fall covered the floor. The stairs were half hanging from the wall and the landing above was about to lurch down. The bedroom that looked over the village was drench-walled with seeped rain. In all the beams there was sign of beetle and in the north bedroom that looked out at Mossymere the ceiling was sagged and blackened.

Joe looked around him. A great iron bedstead had been pushed to the window. Climbing into its frame, Joe scratched at the grease and the fungus on the panes. Piece by piece as a view became clearer, he found that he could see his house in the wood quite clearly. There were trees fallen across, but any lamplight would show for sure. He sat down on the bed, quite obsessed with the realisation that his privacy was stripped away by the view from this one deserted room. It seemed to him that from that very first night he had been naked to the eye of this north bedroom.

He looked around him. The bed had certainly been dragged, not lifted to the window. Its feet had gouged carved grooves an inch deep in the pine boards but that had not stopped its removal. The damage done though was long ago and the dirt lay as thickly in the scars as it did elsewhere on the floor. The fireplace had, however, been relatively recently used. The charred paper there had not broken down and still bore a shiny enough brightness for someone to have warmed himself on a winter's night just gone. Or even on a particularly cold summer's one.

Joe opened the cupboard built in beside the chimney and there remained clothes in a clutch of brandy bottles. He lifted one out but the glass was coated with dust and cobweb laid over long years. The house had no more to offer and thankfully Joe went outside into the near darkness of the overgrown hedgerows. The building loomed up before him, a gaunt affair, tall with ugly brickwork that was probably not older than sixty or seventy years and yet already was close to being a ruin. Joe turned to the village a half mile distant and nearly lost in the gathering mist. He could understand why the blacksmith of those days, once made good, had chosen to leave the village and its whisperings for a place where he could watch, but not be seen, listen but not be heard through the thin cottage walls as the lamps were damped down for the night.

CHAPTER X

Joe admitted to me that the visit to the blacksmith's house had unnerved him and the walk to Mossymere had seemed strangely long. He said he could see a little of what I meant about the wood, its unease, its presence almost like a creature alive. 'I know that once you admit fear at night, that no amount of willpower can prevent hurried glances into the shadows and the demons that spit and grow in your imagination,' he said. He went at once to bed and slipped into troubled sleep.

He woke. It was late in the night and stiflingly warm. He had to go for water. The near full moon was hidden by cloud that threatened thunder. The stairwell was therefore black. He stood in the hall and realised it was the clock that had awoken him. This clock was one of the few pieces of furniture in Mossymere – an old school clock with a large round face and childlike, clumsy numerals, but with key and still working pendulum.

Now, though, its tick was loud, deafening even. Coming out of sleep, he struggled to believe it was as normal, simply amplified by the night silence, but he knew that to be foolish. Even as he stepped out into the yard in search of cooler air, he heard it clearly and even as he listened, it seemed to increase its volume. Its ominous rhythm became erratic. Quick. Quick. Slow, then slower, and then a long pause, a second, two and then the same wild, loud beating once more. To Joe the very heart of the house was in spasm. He lit the kitchen lamp and took it to the clock. His face, wild and tousled, reflected from the glass as he peered at it. The hands shuddered to three and it began to chime. Never before had the hour ever sounded but now the tones were so loud that the devil himself would have heard. At the third stroke, the glass rattled fit to break. And then all was still. The clock had quite stopped. Joe rewound it, but it did not go. He swung the pendulum time after time but once his finger was removed, it fell down limp, like a dead thing.

These events began a period of other nights when Joe awoke around 3 a.m. Sometimes he would gradually drift out of sleep and at others he would jolt upright as if someone had shaken his very shoulder. Always he went for a glass of water and to watch the clock as if expecting it to chime or beat again. Always afterwards, he found sleep impossible. There was a death watch beetle that clicked loud in the roof space above his bed. He could hear rats outside in the long grass and in the yard, hunting in the rubbish there, and once a shed door banged so violently that a dog began to bark in the distant village. He was too tired, he said, to investigate and he was too tired to sleep. He could do little but fall prey to his memories and his illusions.

I moved from my chair and walked to the clock on the wall. I played with it for a while, but quite as Joe had said, it seemed hopelessly broken. Joe had taken the opportunity to pour out yet a further drink: I could see him move furtively in the reflection in the clock face. I chose not to turn round, but I did implore him to leave with me.

'Look, pack your stuff and come back with me. It's no defeat, and don't worry about the book. We can put the thing on ice till next year and choose another wood then. In this mood, damn it in this house – don't you see, Joe, you're doing yourself harm?'

My words were utterly useless. I knew they would be. He

saw me to the car and watched me all the way down the lane. He never waved, but his figure stood there still as I turned into the avenue and out of sight of Mossymere.

CHAPTER XI

Very much later, when Jan told me that Joe had not been home since his return to Mossymere I knew that the wood had encroached on him and entrapped him entirely. After everything that he had told me of Swallow on my visit, I felt that this relationship had to be developing too to keep him away from his family. I was not surprised. His obsession, his passion the day I had met him seemed incapable of check and once Joe's considerable powers were unleashed then I felt sure a country girl would succumb to them. When at last he did return to the city I was invited for dinner. I tried to refuse, knowing Joe and Jan had not seen each other for many weeks, but Joe said he wanted to talk about the book's progress and Jan said privately that my presence would make the reunion a little easier. That thought alone worried me.

The dinner was a muted one. Jan could get little from Joe about either Mossymere or his work. For the first time in their marriage, he had brought home nothing to show her, to share with her. I felt desperately sorry that she who had been so long his first and fiercest judge should now be so ignored. He asked questions about her life without him in a flat, disinterested tone. He showed what concern he could over her problems, but could not become involved in their solution. He was a husk of the husband who had left the weeks before. Even I could see that. His smile was tired and without any warmth. His words were vague and though he was brown from the sun, in certain lights he looked gaunt rather than lean.

Dinner ended abruptly as Jan said, 'Joe, for God's sake if there is anything wrong tell me. Let me help. That's what I'm here for.' Joe looked tired, irritated even.

'Nothing. There's nothing wrong. I've been away, on my own, too long perhaps. I'll adjust in time.'

'But you weren't like this even after Greenland. You hadn't spoken English then for a whole summer.'

'Sorry,' said Joe dully.

'Don't apologise to me. It's just that if there is anything wrong and I can help then do tell me that's all.' Jan had moved close to him as she spoke and placed her hand on his shoulder. Joe shook this hand angrily off.

'Listen,' he said with a quiet menace, a barely controlled fury, 'I am not in need of help and if I were you would be the last person I would come to for it.' Jan's whole body buckled under that. I was horrified both at what he had said and at his indifference to the effect his words had produced.

Jan was crying loudly in the kitchen now but Joe did not go to her. He remained at the table staring into the brandy in his glass as though he were quite apart from the whole scene, as though in mind, heart and soul he were back in Mossymere. I helped Jan clear away the meal whilst Joe never moved. She kissed me.

'Thank you for your help, just for being here,' she said. She approached Joe, but he did not look up and she turned away and went up the stairs. I sat down opposite him at the table. He looked near done to me. He was unkempt, wild and in this modern comfortable house of his, totally out of place. His hair was longer now than I had seen it since his student days. Indeed it could have been the Joe from twenty years back but for the deep lines around his eyes and the tinges of grey threading the sunflecked hair. Certainly, he was as lithe as in those hungry days, but now his energy seemed not so much vibrant and confident as nervous, even destructive. There was an air of desperation about him that I suppose I had sensed but tried not to acknowledge back in the wood.

We both settled over another brandy. Joe was so tired that I offered to leave.

'What's the point man? I won't sleep. I don't sleep there and I'm damned sure that I won't sleep here.'

I had to ask the question, 'Swallow is it?'

'Not totally. I believe now you were right about Mossymere itself. I feel watched there. I can't settle but that doesn't mean I can leave either. In part that's Swallow of course. At least she's a tether of flesh and blood, the one I can see and feel.'

'Do you love her?' I watched Joe carefully and waited long for a reply.

'I'm mesmerised by her. I'd die for her. She's turned me inside out. I'm looking in mirrors again. I'm listening to the stupid words of songs on the radio. I'm living a world of utter romance. I know it. Listen. Today is Friday. I'll welcome midnight because that will bring Saturday and I know that I'll see her on Sunday. See what I mean.' He looked at his watch and said, 'In nine minutes I will be seeing her tomorrow!' He ended the sentence on a note of triumph. He saw the alarm in my face and laughed.

'Don't worry. I'm not nearly as mad as I seem. I dare say I'll see it all through and not hang from a Mossymere beam! So, yes, I do love her. I can't bear to be away from her. The very thought of leaving destroyed a week and now I'm here ruining a weekend for everyone around me.'

'You realise everything you stand to lose?' I asked and immediately regretted the crassness of the question.

'Oh yes, I know that all right. Half of me still wants to deceive, not burn my boat here with Jan. This shirt. All of my bloody clothes I had to get washed by a village woman. They all smelled of Swallow so strong that I still half believe the scent is there.' He tucked his face into the crook of his arm. 'She is in every stitch and every seam, still. It's as though her body is next to me now. I wonder to God that Jan doesn't sense her when she's so real to me.'

Again I made a move to leave.

'Please. Please don't do that. Stay or else what will I do? Do I go up to bed? Hide away in the shadows? Do I lay curled up like a small boy, one who's kissed his mother innocently on the cheek and then turned away into his own dreams? I cannot go to sleep with that woman up there. I simply cannot.' I settled back again and very troubled poured yet another drink. I held it up.

'That's it, Joe,' I said. 'I can't drive now after this one. You've got me for the night now, like it or not.' He gave me a smile I had not seen Joe use before. It was of pure, unaffected gratitude. It was not arch, not controlled, not practised but utterly sincere. After over twenty years, I was seeing something of Joe at last with his defences cast utterly into the wind.

'Can I tell you more about Swallow?' he asked. I nodded.

'We went once to church. Not together. I saw her enter and I followed. I found a seat in the aisle opposite where I could watch her through a gap in the grey heads between us. I could hardly believe the smile on her face when she saw me. There, then, I just knew she loved me. There was a glow around her from a shaft of summer sun through the chancel windows and all the time the parson spoke of the harvest I thought of her. Her face was the brown of the fertile earth. Her lips the poppy red of the headlands. No – don't smile. Don't laugh. I couldn't bear that. Through all that cold building I could feel the heat, the pulse of her breathing and when I prayed, I'll tell you, I begged for her. Standing there even in the eyes of God, I felt no guilt, not even to Jan who has given me everything. What I faced was too big for me to describe. All I could do was to follow where this strange fate took me. I have been driven by it ever since.'

The intensity that he felt overwhelmed us both. I knew there was no answer to this. I had wanted to say that his predicament was to win everything too early in life and to leave nothing for him to strive for in his middle age. Fame, to an extent, fortune to a degree, domestic bliss; to an outsider, these were all his and now it was his death wish to cast them all away. All I replied was, 'Joe, you're beyond help.'

'That's how I want it,' he said. 'No help, no past, no future, no money, nothing but her and the present. I don't want to hurt anyone. I loved Jan, still do, but I can't give her any more. There's nothing left in me for her now.'

'And that's that?' I said.

'Got to be, my oldest friend. It's got to be. You know it. I'm back to Mossymere and never expect me in this damned place again.'

It was well into dawn light before we slept, fully clothed on the chairs, amidst a debris of brandy bottles. It was how many an evening had ended years ago, years before all this damned mess that I felt myself drawn more and more towards.

CHAPTER XII

Joe did go back to Mossymere, of course, and from the evidence I saw later I knew that he still tried to work. From his notes and his letters I also knew a little of life thereafter. Though the book was well behind, though the freshness of summer had nearly run out on him, he was determined to produce photographs still. During that Swancoots garden party in his first days in the wood, Joe had conceived pictures he deeply desired to give expression to.

The lilies of the moat, the arrays of wonderful flowers, the exotic plants and the finest of trees spell promise everywhere to a photographer. He had smelled the most aromatic of shrubs and throughout this Eden were dotted grottos, classical statues and ruins of buildings of an unknown age, now crept over by flowers and ivies. From the moat, a pathway led to a stone bridge over a stream which in its turn splashed into a lake that had sparkled in the light of the setting sun. On the water drifted a golden swan, grazing the luxuriant weed and taking it to his castle-like nest where his mate sat on their chicks. Once their fluff-bald bodies showed as the birds exchanged their duties and Joe yearned for a photograph. Yet, he decided he would leave them until the cygnets themselves were on the water and then he would choose another sunlit evening to frame them in their fantastically ornate and sensuous setting.

And so it was, very early in August, the tripod appeared

on the lawns of the hall, between the bower and willow trees that cascade into the lake there and Joe sat amidst some midges waiting for the sun to settle and the swans to come within range. Nicholas wandered from the hall to meet him. His dress for such an evening, like everything in sight, was exquisite: white shirt, slacks, shoes and straw hat to keep away the flies. The red cravat displayed the vital gash of colour around his neck. As was his custom, Nicholas did not start an immediate conversation, but stood rather like an artist, appraising the scene, looking wise and cultured. He saw himself as a patron, as a man of an earlier age.

For a man in his forties, Nicholas wore his greying hair long, just as he had always done, even when Joe first knew him. Never had the two, neither then nor now, found it easy to make conversation. In that earlier summer, Nicholas had made Joe feel ill at ease, but that was not the case now. Rather, Joe wished they could say more and he found it difficult to decide if the silences, the enigmatic pulls on the endless cigarettes, were profound or a mere papering over of the man's intellectual cracks.

'Those damned swans soil the grass so. Do be careful where you sit.' Joe did not reply and this discomforted Nicholas. He lit a cigarette and angled himself so artfully against a willow trunk that Joe half pondered a photograph of the evening aristocrat. The conversation continued to be humdrum.

'The gardens certainly look fine,' Joe commented.

'I should hope so the money they cost,' replied Nicholas. 'The whole shooting match needs a tribe of gardeners, full-time, to keep them like this. I don't know if it is worth the trouble sometimes, but - well, on evenings like this one does feel somehow charged, responsible, you know, to keep the good things going.'

Joe thought quickly of the silted river, of the tumble-down barns, of the damp dark Mossymere house and the other crumbling, tied cottages that the old, the sick and the children were forced to live in.

'When Lordie, father you know, died,' Nicholas continued, 'I hardly wanted the title or anything of that sort of thing, but these gardens were different. I'm not one for pomp, but I do adore beauty and if we are honest there is nowhere lovelier that I know of.' The neglect of the forest filtered Joe's mind. The decay of ancient oak groves he found far from fine.

'As I say, Joe,' the aristocrat continued, 'and you know exactly what I mean here, we all have a duty towards the environment these days. It's all too easy to let things slip and then there'll be no getting them back again. I can't count the cost when the future is in the balance.'

Joe turned from his cameras and studied Nicholas's face.

'Whatever happened to Ian?' he asked. 'I remember him as one of the best men I've ever known and I couldn't believe how he had gone down.' Nicholas was obviously nervous.

'Well, as you saw, he has taken to drink. You can't have a man like that running the farm.'

'Was he drinking before or after you sacked him?'

'That, Joe, is no concern of yours that I can see. Swallow, I believe, now is, however?' Joe nodded.

'Are you serious about her?'

'Why?' asked Joe.

'Because I'd rather you weren't. Partly for my sake yes, but you're married I know, and I can't see the girl herself benefiting from an entanglement with a man your age. If you go on with this affair I think you'd come to regret it in the end.'

Inside, Joe raged. The interest he had always felt in Nicholas had turned violently to a feeling far more akin to hatred now. He began to pack away his cameras: he had no further desire to record these gardens. Gaudy, shallow, a myriad of colours dragged from every quarter of the globe, he saw only too clearly what Anne had meant the night in the rose garden. He was disgusted now with himself that he, like so many others, had been duped into believing them beautiful. The tripod shut with a snap. He tidied away the bread brought to lure the swans close, drag them into another falsity.

'I didn't realise you'd be finished so soon,' said Nicholas failing to see the anger in the man beside him. 'Don't take what I said as a threat. Just an observation. Believe me. I'm serious. You're not right for each other. It would all end in grief.'

'We'll see. Goodnight then,' Joe replied and, on leaving, a zephyr of evening breeze lifted a hint of aftershave to his nostrils and hung there, mixing with the curl of Nicholas's finest Eastern tobaccos.

'Remember Joe,' Nicholas called, 'a man, or woman, is remembered for what he leaves behind him.'

I don't suppose Joe's anger was rational but during this period of turmoil he found many things hard to order and cope with. He was in no mood by now to brook any checks or criticisms, I know that myself, by his answers to my letters, my pleas for more work, for progress reports, anything.

That night, as so obviously on so many others, he was drunk. Swallow came to see him late, but found him dead asleep and did not disturb him. She moved cautiously around the bedroom, tidied a few of the clothes and left him a note on the dressing table.

He woke only a short while later and smelled her fragrance around the room, not exactly perfume but something attractive he could not quite name. He rose, looked around the house, and saw her bicycle tracks in the sand of the pathway. He was in half a mind to follow her to the village, but he could not decide. He could not be firm about anything any longer. His will had completely gone and he settled for another brandy. By then it was well too late to do anything about Swallow but miss her badly, and sleep or try to sleep once more.

CHAPTER XIII

Hardly ever did Joe use his car that summer. The wood and Swallow were all to him and to leave, even for half a day, was torture. I knew that even if not seeing Swallow he had to feel close to her. On a day of persistent rain, however, he felt the deepest of depression in the cottage. For half the day, he had tried to work and had failed. The silence that I loathed closed in around him and he spent the time pacing from one window to the next, still seeing nothing but the streaming rain. The memory of a wet day there once before grew so strong that he decided to travel to the local town for films and more exotic provisions than the little village shop could supply.

Deep pools had formed in the ruts of the track and he drove slowly, often half on the banking or into the hedgerow. At last though, he locked the last of the gates behind him, stood there for a while looking back into Mossymere and finally nosed the car on to a metal road. Even this was no more than a lane extremely narrow and never more than single track. He hardly expected to meet other traffic but after less than a mile he came up behind an old man on a bicycle. The rider straddled the central crest of green making it quite impossible to overtake. Joe drove close, eager to see more of the decrepit figure before him. His coat was long, misted grimy grey. His hair hung to the collar in locks of dirt and silver. He pedalled with rubber boots badly enough cut for even Joe to see their wear. The old man did not pull in but was well aware of the car on his tail. He glanced in his handlebar mirror, he half looked over his shoulder, but he kept right on with his damnably slow ride. It was three miles yet to anything like a decent road and any patience Joe had ever possessed had long gone. To hell with the tramp. Joe gave a brush on the horn. The rider swayed neither left nor right and, now angry, Joe gave two loud sharp blasts.

The old man swung on his bicycle and turned in the lane towards the car. Joe had to brake sharply but even so there were barely inches more than the bonnet's length between them. The face that Joe now saw was of rage, of evil rage. Oh yes, it was haggard and filthy and old but hate had utterly taken it over. At first helpless before it, Joe began to edge the car past, pressing into the hawthorn, his wheels skidding on the lip of a ditch. As he did so, the old man bent down. He hammered on the glass. He screamed at him in words all but incoherent with anger. The car slowed and stopped a second time, the old man pulled at the handle and the door opened a crack.

'Here agin are ye? Ye bastard. Ye bloody, bloody bastard.' Joe accelerated and the old man was pulled off his bicycle and on to the ground. Still he held on to the car, but, blind with panic, Joe accelerated and the figure dropped away.

In the rear mirror, Joe saw him rise and curse him, dancing on the lane in grotesque fury. It was half a mile before a bend in the road hid the spectre from Joe's sight. He stopped, got out and sank on to the grass. Dislike, contempt, anger Joe had felt before but this manic hatred on the face of an aged stranger horrified him. He felt sick. The words rang just as loud again and again in his mind. So, if he were in Mossymere again, what was that to the old man to cause such wicked concern?

He couldn't drive on. He wandered round the lanes. He made his way back to the wood again. All the darkness, the loneliness flooded back once more at the shutting of the last gate. He drank again in the living room, watching the tired light drop and as the day grew long an explanation began to come to him. Perhaps it was that the face was not unknown to him, but he put the suggestion away as frightening, as absurd and he desperately tried not to think of the incident again. Swallow came fleetingly to visit him and he fought to regain something of his composure, to hide the violence of his emotions from her.

Chapter XIV

By darkness, the rain cleared to show a large and growing moon only a single night before the full. Joe lay in the Mossymere bedroom where there were no curtains, watching tiger streaks of brightness fall across the floor. Dimly he realised he had never noticed a broken pane there – the glass had been put back in and glued once roughly together. As usual he was very far from sleep and once was startled into thinking the telephone was ringing again. It was only a clock tower chiming midnight long, long away. He was cold and went to the pile of clothes by the window and pulled on a shirt.

Once there, he could not leave that view over the moon-bathed wood. A stoat rippled over a silvered length of track. A vixen called close by like a child in pain or terror. Then he saw the figure of a woman watching him from the shadows of the cornfield. But a haze of cloud passed over the face of the moon and the vision melted from his eyes as the shadow faded. It dissolved into his brain, however, as the image of a woman, the one he had wanted so much to be waiting in Mossymere for his return at the start of this strange summer. He felt a growing chill and reluctantly returned to the bed once more.

The sheets smelled of Swallow as if she had only been minutes gone. They were warm after the sharp clear night air. Both this scent and warmth were pleasures so great that her absence stabbed him. He lay, longing to sleep, her presence irresistible, her memory undeniable.

'Swallow, Swallow,' he said over and over. To kiss her. To see her eyes flicker and close as their lips met. To lift her shirt apart, gently, and bow his head to her breasts and to hear her sigh a little and near sob when his kisses reached her belly and the straw brown hair beneath. To feel her whole body relax and fall open to him, her hands on his back, pressing and urging as they made very slow love.

'What devils we are,' she had said, her eyes wide open and glittering in the moonlight.

'I am the devil here, not you,' Joe had replied. Swallow laughed, she had laughed and her whole body had shaken beneath him.

'But I'm your accomplice. I come when you call. I wait for your every sign. If you think you track me, then be quite sure I made a trail clear enough for you to follow. Call me the willing, open-eyed exploiter of your weakness.'

She had stroked his hair. She ran her fingers down his neck and along his shoulders. She picked up his hands and pressed them to her breasts. She arched her back and began to suck gently at his throat. With the tip of her red tongue, she traced the line of his lips.

'And why should there be blame anyway, stupid man? Because you're married? Or because you're twice my age? Because you worry about the end of this? You worry about a wife who doesn't know and for me who doesn't care. So, you are like a summer storm over my head that I know will pass. I enjoy it now, but I would not want it to stay and darken my life forever. I tell myself there'll be sunshine after you're gone.'

They had rolled apart. He watched her squirm like a brown cat beside him.

'So you want me to go then?' he asked.

She replied 'I'm here and I love you and I want you.

That's enough for me and so it should be for you. Enjoy me now while you may.' He was drawn back to her again and again. He could not leave her. He half died when she dressed and left him, alone in the wood.

He could not sleep. He could only watch the moon reveal the hidden life of the forest until a type of tiredness crept on to him and eased him into a fitful half rest.

Chapter XV

Sometime later he was jabbed awake by a moan of wind at the half-open casement. This was sufficiently strong to rattle the pine frame, even though the leaves of the surrounding oaks hung still in perfectly quiet air. I cannot guess what went through his mind as he lay there, tensed for the second breath, the sigh of breeze powerful enough to ripple his shirt cast off at the foot of the bed. This prompted him to rise, put on clothes and cross to the window again. The moon was glaring and just as he knew, there was no cloud, no hint of any end to the total calm of the night.

He fought against a growing thirst for he had no desire to leave that upstairs room for water. His battered logic intervened, however, and soon he stood drinking at the kitchen tap. So strong was the moon that side of the house that there was no need for lamplight. He put down the glass, turned, and was instantly aware of a shadow lying across the floor of the adjoining room. It was the figure of a human, no doubt, for his arm was raised as if to try the window's lock or shield out the panes' reflection from his eyes. Joe pressed into the pool of darkness cast by the separating door. He sensed the intentness of the shadow. It spelled an unmistakable menace and Joe was appalled.

Did Joe now think of some passing tramp or thief? Did he remember the old man with the bicycle and the face of hatred? Did he register any emotion but relief as the shadow moved across the window space and was gone?

Joe stepped up to the window and tried the catch. It was secure, he went further, on towards the door that gave into the sitting room. Here too the shadow lay crucifixed on the moon-bathed floor. Here too he watched his arm raise to try the window panes. The fist now was hammering, but the blows were absolutely silent. Not a sound penetrated the house. Again the shadow moved with stealth away. Now it was passing around to the dark side of the house where there was no moonlight to cast the figure's image. In the back pantry Joe sat on the stills to await the grim identity of the face at the window there. No one came.

Joe went to the outside door and ran around the house. He ran to the head of the lane. He ran into each of the sheds and searched the fringes of the forest. He looked down the avenues and the drives and even as far as the barn up on the meadow. There was no one. There were no footsteps but his own, criss-crossing in the newly-formed dew. He hung there gasping in the chill air. The sweat froze to his brow and he shivered violently.

Indoors, he took up a further glass of water and entered the hall. In pieces the clock lay there, shattered in some soundless fall. Joe was not aware until the broken face gashed his ankle and the blood ran down his bare feet. He returned to the tap to bathe the wound which was deep and long. His watch face caught the moonlight as he worked on the wound. It was quarter past three and he was near despair. His heartbeat filled his temples. The wound still weeped and a chilled sickness grew in his stomach. He had to return to his bed. He stumbled around the clock and lurched towards the balustrade. His outstretched hand filled with a warm liquid. He groaned. He realised that there was blood already on the stairs.

CHAPTER XVI

When Joe did at last fall asleep, it was deeply, lasting until the very late morning. And when he awoke, he found the house in chaos, as though a terrible fight had taken place there during the night. The clock was off the wall and lay with its face shattered. The glass lay dropped and broken. The windows downstairs had been opened and the wind had blown a storm of papers and photographs around the room. Joe's own blood lay caked on to his sheets. There was more on the stairs and on the kitchen sink. He sat listless at the table. His head was in his hands so that he hardly heard the kettle boiling. He was too tired and too uncaring to tidy the mayhem away. The rubble, as far as he was concerned, could stay and stay, if necessary a hundred more years. Images of the night were still powerful and despite the sunlight of another blue day, there were pockets of coldness and rejection that lay in pools of fear around the house.

Joe knew he had to leave the Mossymere house, run free in the warmth and find Swallow. Today was important, was vital he believed, to them both. He had to find her, to take her to some remote part of the forest where he believed the sheen of protection would cover them as they lay. Certainly, he loathed now to be alone in the house. He walked hurriedly to the crest of the downs, past the smith's deserted house, running where the track sloped away, his shirt then blowing like a white sail behind him. Now and then he stumbled in the sand before he came to an oak stump from where he could see the village, the river and Swallow when she would come riding over his heart and across his daylight. He waited there an hour, maybe more until Swallow appeared on the common land, astride the dapple grey mare and guiding her down to the stream to drink. Then he ran and ran across the fields and through the hedgerows to meet her. Halfway, he passed Anne, the art teacher, walking her dog. He slowed down, walked and wished her good-day as they met on the narrow path. She seemed not to recognise him. She did not reply, nor even look at him as they crossed. It was as though he were no longer there before her. Joe paused, followed her a pace and called her name. Now she did turn around, but only to pull at her dog, not to speak or acknowledge him in any way at all.

He and Swallow met at the ford where she dismounted and began to lead the horse by the reins. They kissed. They followed the watercourse to its lake, wading the shallow gravels, kicking the water high in diamonds and crystals that caught the summer sun. When they got to the lakeside, the water was a shield of fire and Swallow turned the horse loose on the pasture there. Free now, Joe and Swallow walked into the reed-mace together, along the narrow planking of an Edwardian landing stage. At the water's edge they slowly, deliberately unbuttoned each other's clothing: there was no restraint between them any more, only a need, a love that they could not even think to deny. They laid the discarded clothes over the planking and the rusted nails and they fell there, where the whispering reeds played above their heads and the water danced to the afternoon breezes at their feet. Swallow's skin was so brown that as Joe kissed it, he said there was the blood of gypsies in her and her eyes, never quite shut even in ecstasy, gleamed white and slits of hazel.

Brown. Brown her hair flowing under her shoulders, over

the strewn clothes. He kissed her thighs, her stomach, her breasts, he wanted to kiss every pore as her fingers played along his back and pulled at his hair, clamping their mouths together. Their bodies bucked and fell against the moss-caked ridge of the staging which threw them back on to their makeshift bedding once more. They nipped, they bit, they stroked, they kissed and they loved again and again as the sun sank towards the alders and willows on the lake's island.

At the last they rolled off the planking into the deep clear water and with the dazzle in their eyes, they swam along the margins. Swallow was now a sleek wet otter brown. Joe, standing on firm gravel, ducked beneath her and held her under the water, arm around her waist. She seemed not to lose breath, but eyes still open, she began to make love there, lying against the stems of the bulrush and the white waterlily. The reeds entwined her body, the bubbles purled in her hair and the silt stirred soft and warm between her legs and on her back. Joe, in torment, fought her, fought for his breath, for a way to live ever more like this. He broke away, through the surface and lay sobbing on the ronde.

Swallow swam out to the island and splashed amongst the alder fingers there, calling out to him across the water. Though exhausted, he followed and waded ashore, to find her under a fountain of silver willow. There they lay till the sun was right down and the starry night grew cold and their breath was hot on each other's bodies. When they slipped into the lake that last time, the water was milky warm around and they stood on the margin and kissed before striking out for the staging that loomed black in the rushes of the far shore. They dressed, made a fire to warm themselves from the ever-encroaching cold and the grey mare came close into the light to graze the meadow around them.

Joe was by now exhausted and Swallow saw it in his face,

in every tired line of his body. 'Am I worth all this terrible bother to you?' she said softly. 'Why don't you leave the wood, the house and me and get back to your normal life again? You can't hang on like this forever. Sometimes I don't know if this is love or an obsession and if we shouldn't try to live apart for a while.' Joe said nothing. He looked across the afterglowing lake. 'I don't want that, Joe, but only if it's best for you would I do it,' she whispered.

Joe replied, 'We are obsessed, I know, I came here to find some feelings and some people all lost to me over the years and I'll admit I've found far more than I ever bargained for. I used to think I was capable and now I'm just lost. Swallow, if you left me now, I don't know what I'd do, how I'd cope. When we're together I feel as if there's a bubble over us, protecting us, and when you're gone you take that with you and I'm vulnerable again. I only sleep when I'm drunk to blot out the stupidest fears or when I'm with you because I feel safe. Perhaps I would go back to a normal life if I could, but right now, I wouldn't know how to begin. Don't you think that's pathetic? Don't I realise you'd be a damned sight better off without me?'

'If I wanted fun,' Swallow said, 'I could find that easily enough, even in a place like this. I don't think you do me a lot of credit and you certainly don't understand what a woman's adoration means.'

Joe, the old Joe, rallied. 'Why I'm pathetic is not enjoying every second with you that God grants me.' He paused. 'Look, what I suggest is a holiday. Why don't we pack a case - tomorrow - get in the car and go to the coast for a week or just however long you can manage away? I've been too much on my own. I've been too far away without other people and what we both need is to escape this wood a while. How about it? A little luxury? I'll even shave once in a while!'

'You promise?'

'I promise.'

Swallow jumped to her feet with a whoop. She capered around the fire. 'I've only got that one red dress you saw me in at Nicholas's party.'

'Then I'll buy you more.'

'Promise.'

'Yes, I promise.'

She continued to dance. 'This is more what I thought taking a rich lover would be like,' she laughed. 'A proper hotel? A private bathroom?'

'I promise,' said Joe.

'Then come mistress mare and let me get you fed,' Swallow called out to the horse. 'Give me some time to pack a case and I'm all yours, wonderful man.'

'Let's say ten tomorrow,' Joe said. 'Do you want to come to the cottage, or shall I pick you up from the village?'

'I'll come to you. There's enough gossip as it is.

Swallow mounted the horse, bent down to kiss Joe and cantered off in the direction of the hall and stables. Joe watched her go till he could see her no more in the dusk and hear the hooves no longer in the silence. He stamped out the embers of the fire and departed in the opposite way for Mossymere.

Chapter XVII

Joe walked into the darkness of the looming forest. He was lame; the wound from the previous night had swollen and though the cool waters of the lake had at first helped it heal, later the sand and rushes had opened up the blood flow again. He felt it trickle warm in his boot and he was glad to be back in the cottage, even though the door still hung open and there was the chaos untouched around. He realised with a dullness that he had not eaten for well over a day; it hardly bothered him, but it did explain his tiredness, his light-headedness, the depth of his bodily ache. Somewhere there was whisky, which he found and took with him up the stairs.

Before long he fell into a deep sleep riddled with dreams so vivid he moved constantly on the unmade bed. The woman he had always wanted, the woman he had come back for was speaking to an older man. She was as fresh and as beautiful as though twenty years had never passed.

'No,' she was saying. 'You're right. We both know this beautiful child I am carrying has nothing to do with you. It's my little love child. I'll call her – for it will be a she, you'll see – I'll call her after the birds.' Joe believed himself awake and looking for his watch.

Somebody was winding the clock – that surely lay shattered on the floor. The sound of the chain seemed distant like this impossible sound of voices. He leaned on his arm to listen.

'You're wrong. I do love him but you're right that he'll never come back. But, if he did, he'd find me waiting. I'll wait forever, you'll see.' Joe recognised that voice and with equal passion he recognised the one that replied.

'He is nothing but a bastard. He will do you no good nor anyone else. Not ever. I'll tell you he'll always float and always cause harm. And me? I've looked after you forty years and I'll be looking after your bastard too till I die.'

Joe left the bed and looked down the stairwell. There was nothing. The full moon made that plain and yet he swore hearing a step on the stairs, feeling a brush on his shoulder, a kiss on his lips that he remembered so well. He felt his hand held. He heard a voice in his ear that said, 'I love you. I've waited. Just please, please come at last for me. I'm not angry, though I've been destroyed.'

Then he heard shouting, anger, and in a gleam of light he believed he saw Maggie's face. His Maggie. Her lovely, lovely face. Finely chiselled. Blood on the lip, blood that oozed, welled and dropped on the stair at his feet. He bent to touch it, to lift her to him, but there was a rough hand on his arm and he looked into the face of the devil, of the old man he had always feared.

His words clashed around and around the stairwell. 'Here agin are ye? Ye bastard. Ye bloody bloody bastard.' Now, there was more. 'See what you've done here? Take Swallow now would yer? So you'd have your own bloody daughter, you bastard?' And as the old man raised his fist, Joe hobbled out, totally naked, into the night.

Part Two

The Student

CHAPTER I

A young man, a student, sat in the hedgerow of the big field outside the hall. He was very tired for the June sun had hardly been up an hour, certainly not long enough to warm the cold soil underneath him. Here and there, stars even hung in the brightening blue sky and a hint of moon, fading, hung in tatty pieces before the might of the coming day. To his right, lay a great wood capped by early mists. Before him, all the way to the east and to the rising sun, stretched the lands of the estate – rich and rolling and so it seemed to him, never ending. He had only known the domain for two weeks and already he was half in love with its acres and its people.

He had been somehow lost in life before his arrival and here there seemed to be a spirit showing him the way. This, then, he could not define and he laughed at himself and paced the headland. He began to kick the potatoes that lay all around him in the fringes of the field. He jogged a hundred paces and ended with a somersault of pure joy. He ran back with the pace of a fast bowler and hurled a fist of potato at a sack draped over the barn wall. It burst apart and set the sparrows under the pantiles a-twittering.

He looked at his watch: he must never do that again as long as this day should live, or it would become immortal, never-endingly long. If he were to survive it, he must forget all his previous concepts of time and sink into the warp that stretched out to greet him. The time that governed the world outside did not exist here in the estate; he had been here long enough to know that these people thought in terms not of months, but of seasons, of years, perhaps of lifetimes even come to that. He had fretted at first when he could not understand that to let an hour go is not necessarily a crime or a waste. Little by little, he was coming to realise that time is relative, subjective, and he was beginning to lose layer after layer of his initial impatience.

True, there were periods of each and every day when he felt close to tears of simple frustration that the sun had not moved quickly, but still hung over the selfsame branch of oak as when he last looked. In the early days he wished himself dead, but not any longer. Like the dust from a storm, from a horse's galloping hooves, he was settling, finding peace, at rest on the earth.

A tall man walked up the rough lane, climbed the gate, scanned the field and smiled when he saw Joe.

'I do believe you is getting better, young man. I'll bet it's not even six yet.' He squinted at the sun a second. 'Five minutes off, I'd reckon, so we're both of us early it seems. Join me for a bite of breakfast.' Joe pulled up a sack next to the giant, Ian, the farm manager, but a working man still. They shared a sandwich of cold sausage, coarse, filled with onion and garlic that would lurk on their tongues every hour of the coming day. Joe blew his clouded breath into the palm of his hand and recoiled. Ian had watched him and laughed.

'Let's get the machine together, hey?' Work had begun.

The fifteen-hour, rather the sunrise to sunset day, stretched ahead of him and Joe was able to accept it now, as a gift, as a security. His life was perfectly ordered at the command of this big man. The machine was the yellow ship of the potato field; the harvester. Vast, billowing with canvas, a structure of pulleys, conveyors, shoots, plough shears and timbers that creaked as it rode the furrows behind its tractor. In minutes, Ian would drive it, four women would take to the conveyor belts to sort the potatoes coming through the machine, and Joe would stand on the boards beneath to sack and stack the hundredweights of flowing vegetable. Ian greased the nipples of the leviathan and Joe knew that his back would lift tens of tons of potatoes before the night pulled in.

A truck stopped at the gateway. Four women stumbled over the rows: the team of six was now complete. There was some talk, a little laughter drowned by the growl of the engine and the clatter of the yet empty belts. The women clambered aboard, one fat, one thin, all grey but one: Maggie. She took the end position as a potato was dropped at last for Joe to sack. Hers was the point of utmost responsibility. Any green, rotten or blighted potatoes discovered at the markets would be for her to explain. She never had to. She was excellent. She had fingers that flew, eyes that danced, a humour that played the hours away, and intelligence that shone. Between them, Maggie and Joe, they were invincible. Ian said he had never known such a team and because of them, the machine never stopped for any accident or spillage. Day in, week out, the two of them earned the whole crew their bonus and they were roundly praised for it by all. Those few extra coins would be special in the winter-time when Joe would be gone back to college and the summer dream would be drifted away.

This morning, like all those preceding it, was soon warm, and by their first stopping time, hot. Joe's shirt was already off and his sweated back was coated with a film of dust and dirt. The scent of fresh earth enveloped them all as they sat in the shade of the big oak. Their faces were grimed by the four hours' work and, for Joe, there was at least double that still to go. By midday, the sunburn was beginning to show even through the soil on his shoulders and at lunch, Maggie washed him in water from the horse drink and rubbed cream into the redness. The other women whistled and Ian told him to look out! Joe and Maggie laughed and kissed passionately before the audience. There was great applause and Joe's mouth burned on into the afternoon.

In the early days, there had been boredom and a realisation of the vastness of the day yet lying ahead. Now he had learnt to watch the sun, accept its blazing journey and sing all the songs of beauty he had ever heard to help it on its way. He could hum, roll them over and over in his head and replay the times that he had heard them sung; darkened rooms, walks in parks and blue eyes, catlike in his. Now Joe was with Maggie, with them all, at one with the machine, adjusting his pace, living the inevitability of snail time.

This day was perfect to him. He smelled in it a replica of the last year, a forerunner of the year to come and on after that when many such days would follow. He saw himself in a whole lifetime of such days, wanting no novelty, no change, no separation from the soil and the sun. I suppose for the very first time, Joe was in love, in awe of something far too large for him to understand. Just to glimpse it was enough. Maggie smiled at him. Her fingers played on his back to sense his soreness and she said goodbye.

It was the late afternoon; the women left and their place was taken by four old men from the estate. The work instantly became slower. They made mistakes and constantly called Ian to stop and let them sort their rotten potatoes. Joe was not sorry. He had lifted ninety tons already and he had four, perhaps five hours still ahead of him. His back glowed from the sun, from fatigue and from the bites of diamond-eyed horseflies that relished his hot blood. So be it, he thought, the sun is on its way and the evening is shadowing in. Now midges were curse enough to force on his shirt and light the pipes of the old men so vigorously they all worked in a fog of smoke. On one hundred and ten tons, the machine began its homeward row. Ian held up his single index finger and the day was all but done. Within a turn of space, the old boys were on their bicycles, cranking away into the gloom. Their lamps bounced off the trees and startled a pheasant roost. Their voices, the rattle of their saddle-bags, the tinkle of their bells drifted a long while through the air and then, finally, they were lost.

Ian began to tidy the machine, to straighten the pallets, and to stack the last of the potatoes. Joe helped to the end, though he did not have to, rather because he enjoyed the peace and the cool.

'Come back to supper,' said Ian, when all was done. 'I'll be on my own most likely and I'd like company.' Joe was pleased to agree; he had no need for bed, no food prepared, no one waiting, nowhere much to go but for the estate cottage put aside for him.

Together, they walked the fields to the farmhouse, exercised Ian's dogs in the last of the light and settled down to a cold meal waiting on the table of the kitchen. Ian threw huge shadows from the lamps but then in life he was a colossus. There was a note by the food. He skimmed it and threw it on to the fireplace.

'There's no problems in life but women, lad,' he said and nodded to the grate. 'Says she doesn't know when she'll be home tonight. A dawn job again, I suppose. We met in the yard this morning, her coming in and me going out to the field. I wonder to God why she gets up at all, why she doesn't stay all night with the bloke. I'm past caring about any of it. I found her knickers one day in her handbag and I worried for days what they were doing there. And when I worked it out, that did for me. I couldn't be buggered about her no more after that.'

Joe sat quiet, lost in front of all this honesty, this devastating opening of a near-stranger soul. It was his first ever knowledge that such a mighty figure could be so lost, that any universe so secure could be so unhinged. So these were the tangled thoughts that dominated the driver's head all the long day.

They ate in silence a while until Joe replied, 'You work too hard, Ian. You're a slave here. You never rest, you're out all hours, checking, worrying, working. You're only the manager here and in the end you'll see they won't value you for it. You'll be thanked and forgotten.' Ian had stopped eating and sat hunched in his chair. 'I'm sorry,' said Joe. 'I don't know really. I had no right to say all that.'

The older man shrugged his heavy shoulders. 'You see, don't you, I'm into middle age. Emotionally I'm almost done, spent, you know. It's all downhill for me so what else is there, hey, if I don't work? I'd rather be busy than alone here in this bloody barn of a place, wondering where she is, what she's doing, if she'll be home. Work's no problem to me, lad. Just her.'

CHAPTER II

What could stop the giant wheel of life here was human or mechanical frailty. A cog could bend. A belt could snap. A pivot could jam and the whole galleon of the machine would grind to a halt, becalmed in the doldrums of potato plant green. The bonus slipped inexorably away with the track of the sun. The spark of bad temper then could kindle the barely hidden tiredness and the heat, the dust could explode the whole keg of passion. One late summer day, Joe's own patience was tested beyond his youthful endurance. It was a period of crackling, dry heat that brought the tiny, black, biting harvest flies out of the corn in their billions. All day, they had colonised his entire semi-naked body and yet so intense was the work that for twenty minutes at the time, they tortured him without any fear of reprisal or removal.

By late afternoon, Joe's nerves jangled and hung raw and in every crevice of his body irritation crawled. At change-over, the oldest of the ancient men, Lennie, failed to appear. Maggie stayed on; as the youngest by far, and the strongest, it was expected of her. What she thought when only the three bicycles appeared, Joe did not know. He watched her face acutely and she blew him a kiss and swept the harvest flies from her own mane of sun-bleached hair. Then shadows fell once more and she was pools of light and dark above him.

An owl called early from Mossymere wood but there was

no sign of Ian's fingers signalling the end of Joe's personal torture. In the dusk, the boards were a dangerous place to work and Joe walked the tightrope of a hundred snags and snares, arrogant in his youth, his ability and his strength, but tired, smiling a time too often at his angel Maggie above him. He cut his thumb. The ball ripped on a nail, the flesh parted like a peach and all down a row his blood spotted the boards a rich ruby red. At the headland, he was forced to stop despite the obvious anger of the old men. Maggie led him to the hut to tend the wound.

She examined it in the lamplight and, deciding it wasn't worth stitches, sluiced it in cold water a while. The machine had started a new row, going slow, an old man on the board, the two cronies spread out on top of the belt. Little by little, it edged off into the dusk and Maggie turned down the lamp. She went to Joe, lifted his hand, took the aching thumb into her mouth and began to suck the thumb clean. Her eyes never left his face as she licked and suckled the swelling wound. Joe kneeled down before her, his eyes now level with hers, their heads only inches apart. There they remained until she gave up the thumb with a final kiss and with her strong, brown hand took his fingers from her shoulder and replaced them on his own knee. She reached out, lifted him upwards and took a single step forwards. As he stood there, she met him full on the mouth and he tasted the salt of his own blood on her breath. There was a smear of him on her cheek and with his moistened lips he kissed her clean. Her body pressed firm against his a second only. She threw back her shock of hair, kissed him a last time, left him and the hut and walked the gold-dusted field to the returning machine.

'He'll mend,' Joe heard her call to Ian. 'Let's get on with it. I'll do his job on the boards a while and Henry can get back on the belt.' And so it was that as the moon rose, Maggie worked in the coming night just as well and as unfalteringly as the student himself. Joe watched her lithe strong body bending, lifting, stretching, so utterly capable of fending anything the world could throw at her and little by little, he was further entranced.

The shift ended. She walked strongly away into Mossymere without any look, any goodbye. The apricot moon was well high and in the dell, a nightingale sang. Joe's urge was to run and follow her, but he was half afraid of her, of the wood and of a life he knew so little of.

'You did right to let her go,' said Ian. 'Get you on home. Get to sleep and put all that aside. You're too young to understand a woman like Maggie.' The last of the old men had gone when Joe looked a first time at his watch. It was so late that he made a bed in the hut of sacks and pallets and slept feeling as close to Maggie as it was possible for him then to come.

CHAPTER III

One day heavy rain stopped the harvest until late afternoon and Joe was sent off into the Mossymere forest on an errand. He returned shortly after lunch when the rain had cleared to find the farmhouse in flood. The little round farm pond, generally no deeper than the average duck, had taken the deluge from the field, held it up and then burst its banks with terrible consequences for the house. By the time that Joe had arrived the wave of water had long gone along the ditch to the lake at Swancoots Hall. It had, however, passed through the house on its way and left a seal of glistening mud behind it, trekked by tiny toadlings and newts, swept from the brook and the pools shallows. There were water insects pathetically marooned, dragging themselves on the browned skimmed pamment tiles. There was a roach breathing its last by the old cooking range, but there was no sign of any farmhand, let alone Ian. There were only bootprints in the sludge.

Joe followed them through the winding passages, into room after field-soaked room until he came to the massive front hall. The great door was opened, presumably to let the inundation free, and there was Ian, profiled by the now bright day without. Joe saw with a shock that he stood there in tears, his Goliath's body, shaking, sobbing, strangely noiseless: Joe waited for some minutes: Ian did not move: he continued to look out into the yard, his shoulders heaving, his hands like great paws daubing at his moist eyes. With half a mind to slink back into the shadows, Joe ultimately decided to do what he could. He sloshed to the doorway and said 'Come on old boy, we'll all be able to sort this mess out. Don't bother yourself about it to this extent. The old house will have seen worse in its life I'll promise you.'

Ian turned, and laughter choked through the tears, 'No damn it Joe, it's not that. A bit of mud never hurt no one, least of all me. I don't blubber over nonsense. It's just, just, oh bugger me, look at that.' He pointed out to the scum-coated gravel of the yard. All Joe could see was the destroyed flowerbeds and the flood of brown as far as the white five-bar gate. Ian saw his lack of comprehension. 'No, look at all that.'

Joe swung his gaze in closer only feet from the porch. In the dirt lay a confetti of photographs; Ian as a boy, Ian as a young man, Ian on his wedding day, Ian in front of the big farmhouse. 'I'm soft Joe. I was crying at all that. Somehow it just seems that's all there is left of me.' Joe sent Ian back into the kitchen, returned to the porch and gathered up the flotsam of his shipwrecked life.

The gang was called up for a late shift. They walked across the damp field to where the machine was waiting, Joe and Maggie a little in front of the three old men.

'I met your husband today,' Joe said. Maggie looked straight ahead in silence so he continued, 'Your house is the most lost, wonderful place I've ever seen. What's it like to live there, never seeing another light at night, in all that silence, all that wood? Aren't you ever scared there?'

'I'm never alone there,' she replied, 'and though there are strange things about that house, I'll admit, I'd never leave it. I was born there in Mossymere and I'm quite content to die there someday. It's what I know and if my spirit roams there one day then I'll be glad.' She smiled and said more seriously, 'Why you're really puzzled is that my husband is so much older than I am. But you're too polite to ask, aren't you?'

'Well, I did notice.'

'You wouldn't understand if I did tell you, Joe,' she said. 'He was a road mender, the Lengthsman they called him then, for the estate before he retired. I remember him working from when I was a little girl. He took me with him and I sat in his barrow with his shovel, his hammer, his pick and all his tools – his lunch even. He pushed me miles, telling me stories and I'd look up and adore him. In summer he'd bring me home white with dust and in winter half drowned with rain and mud. He was everything to me then as a child.'

They reached the machine and Maggie swung up. They were still ahead of the others, Ian was linking up the tractor and for a second they were hidden by the canvas. She took his hand and said very quietly, 'I owe him a great deal. He is very dear to me. You must remember that, even if you don't know the rest.'

The sunset night was on fire and every look she glanced him was a flash to last over twenty years. But what did this fine woman owe to the old man Joe had stumbled on to in the drenching wood? He looked at her worn clothes, her hard-worked hands. He saw in her a woman who could have had everything and done everything she might have ever wished. Her beauty, for he was sure she was truly beautiful, her strength and intelligence were every bit as apparent to him as the stars appearing above and yet what could there ever be for her but long hours of work in the summer and days of damp and grey in the winter? Two lovely eyes in the shadow of the awning: condemned to a life with a companion old enough to be her father. How could she be buried alive in the Mossymere forest and not fight, not struggle to leave and live her own existence? Although Joe could master days now he was utterly unable to come to grips with lifetimes.

At the end of the evening shift, Maggie walked her usual path homewards into the wood. Joe could see her until she came to a plank bridge over the stream and then she was lost in the dusk and the alders.

'Maggie,' he murmured after her. 'Tell me, tell me I'm right. He's a king and you're a princess and all this is your kingdom to come!'

Joe and Ian returned to the farmhouse and between them, quite alone, they had shovelled away the mud and washed the floors and made everything good again before the first traces of dawn broke.

Chapter IV

On a Friday lunch, Joe went to the hall at Swancoots to collect his wage. Nicholas, the heir to the domain, took him to one side and congratulated him on the bonus.

'You're the best summer worker we've ever had here,' he said.

'I enjoy the job and I like to do it well,' Joe replied to a man five, perhaps ten years, his senior. 'And I need money for next year.'

'Would you like to earn a little extra tomorrow night, then?' asked Nicholas. 'Could you come here at eight to serve drinks at my little . . . my little cultural evening?' He blushed very slightly. 'It's the first time anything like this has gone off at the hall and I'd like it to be a success.' The idea appealed at once and Joe accepted.

'You'll need a black tie and suit so take this afternoon off to get fitted out.'

'What about Ian and the machine?'

'I'll square that. Can you take Maggie to town with you? She's in charge of the coats and has nothing better than pig sacks to wear.' Joe's heart soared.

He quivered while Nicholas and Ian argued over the depletion of the potato gang. The last tons of the working week were vital and to lose both Joe and Maggie would slow the machine impossibly. Everyone, Nicholas included, knew that, but from the very start Ian was going to be defeated. He left the courtyard an angry, beaten man and for a second Joe felt treacherous to his chief; but the afternoon was safe.

On another sun-shot evening, Joe stood tall and elegant on the drawbridge, welcoming the countryside's dignitaries as they entered the great stone building. Maggie was behind him in the porchway, taking coats and hats as required. She wore black too and her fair hair shone. The fabric clung to her tightly, around a slim waist, barely cloaking the most powerful of feminine bodies. Joe looked at her again and again, in total awe, admiration of this woman who seemed only half tamed, at least half wild. Seeing her now, manicured and shining, only highlighted her inherent savagery, her abnormal beauty that held him and fascinated him. And frightened him. He heard two men murmur, 'What a striking woman,' as they passed and he knew that his love was not blind. Often, Joe saw open amusement on Maggie's face. Her life could not be more different from these rich pampered ladies now around her but it was evident she saw little to be envious of.

Drinks Joe served with buoyant panache. His spirits were somewhere up on the sunbeams and he showed off to the fair lady with him – as Joe was always wont to do. Excited by the occasion, his clothing, Maggie's presence, the whole sparkling evening, his exuberance was unquenchable.

The programme began: two uncomfortable men and a faded woman sang snatches of opera. Forgettably. Not now required, Joe and Maggie settled into a far, dark corner of the hall with a bottle of red wine and the music washed around them there cradled within the granite walls. Performer followed performer and there was a great deal of dullness: recitals, chamber music, a quavering songstress and all the while the audience grew more soporific in the big chamber. The lights were switched on which only increased the heat and embarrassed some of the old out of sleeping in the shadows.

And yet the whole evening was not to be lost. Herbert Walker was in the wings, drinking heavily it is true, but still very much upright. Herbert Walker was Nicholas's ultimate attraction, the reason for the large attendance, for the whole night in fact. Herbert Walker was then surely the country's greatest living poet. Not one of the audience had failed to watch for him. Everyone felt awe, and gratitude to Nicholas who alone had managed to lure the celebrated recluse to the platform. His reputation, both intellectual and personal, was immense and magnetic: a heavy drinker, the father of dozens of children, a hell-raiser in war-time New York, husband to several wordly and wonderful women, Herbert was a dangerous man to have in the house and yet his greying face spoke of nothing but benign calm.

Joe had already poured him many glasses of wine and yet was pressed to unearth a bottle of whisky. Elizabeth, the last and the wonderfully dark-eyed wife, watched with mounting alarm. She signalled hurriedly to Joe as the bottle passed Herbert's way again but the enraged poet seized the glass and poured his own death-defying measure. A short intermission followed a lady with violin and Joe made his final round as drinks man. There was a busy expectancy and then a wave of hush as Nicholas rose to introduce the great man.

'We're all proud that Herbert Walker has chosen to live with us on this estate now his days of travel are perhaps done. His works adorn my study walls just as I know they do yours and everywhere they are much read and greatly adored. Is there anyone who can ignore the poignancy, the power of these my favourite lines?' Nicholas drew himself up tall and with a flourish recited the opening stanzas of 'My Grandfather'. He was met with riotous applause.

'Thank you! Thank you!' he said. 'But I know the praise

is not for me but for the land's greatest modern poet. Ladies and gentlemen, the time has come and I give you Herbert Walker.'

The great hall rang as valiantly as if the conqueror at Agincourt were coming home and the ladies of the front rows actually stood and cheered as the befuddled poet clambered to the rostrum. He swayed a very little and reached into his pocket for the verses he had prepared.

'Screw 'em. They're on the kitchen table,' he said. A quite audible groan was heard from Elizabeth and she ran hurriedly to the front of the room.

'I'll get them. We're only a minute away.' Desperate, she finished, 'I'll be back ever so soon.' She fled into the velvet night.

'Boy,' Herbert roared, 'bring that blasted scotch up here. I'll improvise till the bitch gets back here.' Nicholas stirred uneasily, yet nodded to Joe. Herbert had seen it all. His presence was now massive, compelling. His face swollen, his hair long and haggard but his eyes were still bright and his speech cuttingly clear. The whisky had worked a magic on him and the wild man was out.

'Bugger him, lad. Bring the scotch or I'll be damned if I'll say a word."' Joe gave him the bottle. The torrent poured from the neck down the craggy throat and Herbert began to talk.

'In New York, I lived with a whore - a Brazilian. A dancer. A woman of puma slit eyes with the strength of tigers and the grace of leopards. Her hands were always bejewelled, fingers like claws, powerful, sensitive, sublime, and she knew how to handle a man, how to drive him insane with desire before she gave him satisfaction. I'll tell you, every man she provoked with her mouth, her eyes, her breasts and her music. This was a woman I loved and I'll tell you again there was not one part of her body you bastards wouldn't have died for.' Joe was fascinated by the old man;

he leaned over the balcony, drawn by this description of a savage from another continent and another age. In the depth of his passion he believed Maggie was the woman Herbert described.

'When we gave parties, I took off her clothes for all to see . . .'

There was a sudden swell in the audience. Chairs scraped backwards, in their ones, twos and in whole rows the audience flocked to the doors as though a fire were at their heels. Nicholas attempted a second to hold them back but was swept aside in the perfumed tide. Elizabeth met the flood and threaded through it into the chamber.

'There you are, cow,' called Herbert. 'I've been giving the sods a bit of my old impromptu. I was coming to the piece where Jewel ran off with that black woman. And what none of us knew, she was a dyke anyway!'

Elizabeth paled and she reached for the nearest support: a delicately-legged eighteenth century side table. Shell-like, it collapsed under her weight, shedding the porcelain it bore like hail on to the marble. Nicholas seized her as she fell. He was screaming now.

'Get out. Get out and take that miserable old drunk with you. Never, never, never do I want to see you or him anywhere again. Never. Just leave. Go. Get out!' Elizabeth gathered Herbert and their injured dignity, and together they swept from Swancoots forever.

CHAPTER V

Before the rush, Joe and Maggie scampered from the hall to the summerhouse on the edge of the lake and sat in there a while with the very last bottle of wine they could find in Swancoots. The night was wonderfully bright and the swans glowed silver on the moonshot water. There was a nightjar behind them in the thick aldercar and bats flickering in and out of the old thatched building. Here and there were lights in the night as the last of the evening's guests made their hurried way home along the tangle of narrow lanes.

Joe looked away from the water, from the glittering hall to his companion; she was already watching him. He reached out for her and she came towards him. He held gently on to her shoulders and she did not move. His hands moved down her back and she pressed herself to him. She shivered slightly, but then the night was clear and already cold. They did not kiss, talk, or even watch the other's face. Simply, they were content to hold each other, part in passion, largely overwhelmed by the relief that the bond between them could be expressed. Secretly, each had dreamed of this moment all summer long and now it had come. The floodgates were being winched up and the flow of desire began to trickle through. It would eventually well and burst with irresistible force. Joe said that they realised that then, both of them.

They were disturbed by a violent argument. Two figures

appeared on the lawns: Nicholas and his father, both walking quickly, voices high and at times shouting.

'Tonight should be a lesson to you,' the older man said, furious. 'Get your mind on the estate and forget all your bloody pretensions of greatness. You've made us a laughing stock tonight. This farce will be round the county by tomorrow. Oh, you bloody, bloody idiot.'

'I hardly see it was all my fault. I didn't know what a moron that Walker could be. You knew better than I did and you did bugger all to stop him, did you? I think you're half pleased the evening's failed. Now you can tell me to get down to the potatoes, to wheat and stinking pig slurry. Well, I warn you, when this estate is mine I'll make it a byword for beauty in all the county, do you hear? The thing is I've got vision and you haven't. You're just an old farmer and there you stop.'

'When you get hold of this estate it will be a disaster. It will be bankrupt in no bloody time. If I could think of a way round it, I'd make sure you never inherited.'

'Well you can't and you know it. I'll make something of this place over your dead body one day.' There was silence and the two men stared angrily into the water. Nicholas began again.

'I'll tell you something else, I'm not pleased with that boy, Joe, the one who did the drinks. He did nothing to stop Walker having a skinful either. He's supposed to have some sense but he left it well hidden tonight.'

'That's your fault again,' said Lordie. 'Anyone can see he's infatuated with the Lengthsman's wife. There'll be trouble there in the end and you'll hardly help by throwing them together in fancy clothes and a wine bath. If you notice, they've both cleared off together now, hey? I wouldn't trust that old man if he finds out. He'll kill the lot of us ...'

The voices trailed away the far side of the hall. Joe and

Maggie still stood together, but the joy had cooled around them.

'Maggie, there's a lot I don't know about you.'

'My lovely man, there is and don't ever think of trying to find out.'

CHAPTER VI

The day following was a Sunday and, of course, there was no work on the estate and therefore no chance or excuse to see Maggie, locked away from Joe deep in Mossymere. In the afternoon, Joe wandered to the farm to ask Ian permission to fish for eels in the pond there and together they entered the orchard to dig worms for bait.

'I used to dig here as a boy,' Ian said. 'The ground's never disturbed you see and those windfalls that rot make the earth good and rich. I used to get lobs like pythons in those days.' They dug for an hour, shirts off, and amassed a pail full of shining worms. Far too many Joe knew, ever to be used, but there was never any stopping Ian once he was embarked on a task.

'That'll be enough now for sure,' Joe had said a dozen times. Always the same reply, 'It won't hurt to get a few more. The old wrigglers might really be on tonight when it gets cooler. It would be a shame then to find you'd run out of bait. You'll have a killing, boy, believe me! Bugger me, we haven't got half enough worms yet.'

So it was late afternoon before Joe finally set up, beside the little pond, alive with hatching flies and the flipping of tiny roach and carp. He hooked on two of the hugest worms, cast them into the centre of the pool and watched the rings spread back to the grassy bank where he sat beneath the poplar trees. There was not a sigh of wind in them and not a breeze stirred the scum-laden surface of the pond. In the oppressive heat Joe lay back, half asleep, half aware of the piping kingfisher jetting blue, of the geese pecking in the pail and the red float lying becalmed in the reflection of the farmhouse. He heard Ian's wife leave and there were no goodbyes. He saw Ian take his dogs on the last round of the estate and return an hour later when the sun had dropped to rest on the ridge of the barn roof.

They settled around him, man and dogs watching his float and the swallows skimming the pool.

'This is utter peace,' said Ian, and indeed it was: one of those golden evenings when perfection can be seen close to, when all the combinations of the universe lock together and the safe door to paradise clicks open at last.

'I half feel glad the wife's gone, you know,' he continued. 'I hate the bickering and all the bad looks there'd be if she looked out and saw me relaxing here now.' He turned his face up at the eastern sky where sprinklings of stars were already appearing and said, 'I like to see those. They put all the silliness to one side - make me believe that life is fated anyway and there's not a jot of good worrying about things one way or another.'

Joe again felt awkward to be with the estate manager in this mood, but he was content to listen, passive, a gnome by the giant's fish pond. His float was on the move now. It bobbed, rose, veered to the left, swung to the right, curtseyed and lay flat. Joe reeled the line tight and prepared to strike.

'Give it a minute longer,' said Ian and when the float again cocked, moved fast into the centre of the pool to disappear there, he whispered urgently, 'Now!'

The eel thrashed the pond to foam and whipped the water to the colour of gravy. It sought refuge in an old sunken cart and then under submerged branches, but Joe kept on an unforgiving pressure that soon had the creature lying in the dew-soaked grass. It was two feet long and thick as its captor's wrist. Its mouth gaped for air and its eyes glittered in the last of the light. Ian was triumphant.

'Yes, we've got the old bugger. He'll do the whole lot of us for supper tonight – yes, you dogs and all. He'll have been in here for years, I'd guess. Just by looking at the size of him. That's what I mean by fate, Joe lad. He was just waiting for you to come here and catch him. We're all helpless before it, you see.'

Ian severed the giant eel's head and the body writhed a last time by the side of his long-time home.

'And what you don't know yet Joe lad, is that life is more often cruel than kind.' Ian prepared the eel expertly. He hadn't lived by the little mere forty years for nothing. The fish was skinned, diced and fried. They ate it later, cold with beer, a little before midnight.

'This is the biggest eel I've seen for years,' Ian said. 'Ever since that cold winter – '47 or '48 it was – say anyway about twenty years back. The little old pond froze solid it did. The eels lay all around the margins as they died. We made belts of some of the buggers. They was forty-eight inches long I'll promise you, forty-eight inches long.'

As they were dividing out the meal Ian held some of the eel back.

'There's a girl around here that loves cold eel', he said. 'I'd keep her a piece if I were you.'

'Maggie?' asked Joe and Ian nodded.

'You must know her well,' Joe said and Ian grunted.

'All her life I've known her – from a little girl to a proper woman. I know her as well as anyone on the estate – we played together as children when she really was a wild one I'll tell you.'

Ian was quiet for a while. He rose and paced the kitchen, fetched a bottle and two glasses.

'Damn it, Joe. It's us three that are keeping the machine

on the job. If us two are late tomorrow, they'll not start without us. Or her. Maggie. Maggie as a child – I just can't tell you how wild she was. She could run. She could fight. She could climb any height. Control her? None of us could. She'd fall and you'd see no tears. She was lovely then. Every limb of her. Did we love her then? Us all, never you fear that boy.'

The bottle began to pass round quickly. The glasses sparkled and danced in that vast room where the giant sat, spilling his heart out and his woes. He sat at the table, head in hands. No fire in the grate this cold summer's night so that Joe put a jacket on, drank his drink, prepared to sleep there on the bench. The man's mood darkened. He began to shout.

'Night times she was out. She flew the woods here and there. Going nowhere where she should be. She robbed the keeper. Took the pheasants that no one else ever dared. She didn't care! In truth, Joe lad, she ran wild, like a hare.'

Joe sat back, poured a drink, kept his tongue, not for him to butt in. Ian, eyes wide, memories in flood, 'There came a time, the keeper, the new man there, said it was only right to solve the crime. He got us together, the older lads and set us to keep the watch. Come one night, I, yes me, saw her on the ride. She'd nowhere to hide. We chased her like a fox. All through Mossymere she led us a dance – I didn't think we stood a chance. Then she crossed a bridge, slipped off the side and we were there.' Ian began to breathe deep and slow. He poured another drink.

'Not a one guessed a girl, lying there, spitting, our minds awhirl whatever to do. One wanted to cut her hair and I bloody well said shoo to him. That, or it would come to fighting. Yes, I said, didn't I, the girl was wild?' He leaned over close to the boy, 'But she was still a child. I tell you, Joe, she looked into my face and I saw hatred overflow. Even later when we could have been lovers, that's right, that blasted chase always kept us apart a pace. Why didn't we marry ... God knows? I blame that damn night. Things between us ... well we could never get them right.' The hour slipped towards one.

'We took her back to the Lengthsman. Her family was dead or gone. And now you know her soul. Her past. We both know we love her.' Ian fell quiet. The whisky was low. That flight of fancy was over. His simple bitterness showed. 'Why I married that woman here when I once could have had Maggie I'll never know.'

By now both men were very tired.

'But why did she go and marry that old man, the Lengthsman as they call him?' asked Joe.

'That you'll have to ask her, Joe, not me.'

'Would she tell me then?'

'You don't think your love is on its own do you? I'll tell you, I know Maggie better than anyone and I know what she feels for you. So don't go forgetting that piece of eel now. Take it home and be damn sure to bring it to the field with you in the morning.'

CHAPTER VII

Only once that summer did Joe contact me and that, I felt, was unwillingly. We had made brave plans to travel into northern Italy once we had worked and saved money but as the time passed I feared they would come to nothing. I waited as long as I dare, then wrote to the estate demanding if I had a companion on the adventure or not. Joe's reply was unexpected: I have it still. He told me he was learning all he ever needed on the estate and far more about love and beauty than the glories of Venice, Florence or Padua could ever impart. There were all manner of passions he told me, that he had never realised before. Though he had been in love, he had never glimpsed past the one dimensional nature in that affair. Now, he said, he was on the threshold of a dream.

The summer was alive with influence on him and it appeared that he had a sage, a mentor. Joe described him as a dreadful, drunk, wicked old man who lived on the fringe of the village in a decrepit mansion by the river. There, midst mists, fine poplars and wild orchards the man wrote poetry of great beauty and talked to Joe of his life, his loves and his beliefs.

Joe found the old man not happy, not contented but yielded to a type of acceptance.

'Call it a ripeness,' Joe wrote. Never before had the poet wanted to stay in one place, but had always moved, city to city, culture to culture. Now however he was seemingly anchored in the estate. He told Joe it was a good place to be. He helped to crystalise all the unfocused thoughts and feelings that Joe himself was beginning to appreciate. He confirmed Joe's belief that there was a spirit quite special and unique around the estate, but would not name it or describe it. He said that it was for Joe to discover for himself and make of it what he could.

I have no doubt that the poet's influence over Joe was very strong. Joe always wanted to be an artist of some sort, a creator, as this old man genuinely was. I imagine Joe sat, listening, always hopeful of catching some of the sparks from this great man's fire.

In the letter Joe wrote a disturbing paragraph on the joys of sexual love: I do not know why I found it worried me, perhaps simply as an indication of how far Joe was moving out of my orbit, into a cosmos where I could not follow, physically or intellectually.

'Sex,' he wrote, 'must be mixed with the whole range of emotion if it is to mature, to develop, to explore the wide horizons within us from the heavens to the hells. To flower, to blossom, sex has to mingle with mystery and magic, the new and the novel, with love and with laughter. All senses must be aware and heightened. Skin changes texture, hair tints in different lights: exploration and appreciation are everything or physical love dries, dustlike, moist as the desert at high noon. You must wander between fear and comfort, intellectual excitement and bodily lust, joy and tears, and realise no relationship should be an atom less static than the sky above you in a vivid April storm. Passion,' he said, 'is a child of the wind and a harvest of the sun first and then the rain, and even the frost, clearing the soul as it does the winter earth. Passion should run all the rapid changes from heat to cold from light to dark back to dazzling heat again.

'Age is an irrelevance, like race or looks even. My poet's wife is many many years younger than he and yet she is in an earthly bliss. No, no that is ridiculous, for what she has indicated of her life reveals how banal and humdrum the texture is of our own. My love now, here, too, is one decade, perhaps two, my senior but that would be the last of my worries. What would destroy me would be the lack of pain, or promises, of hopes and of bitten back, tongue-tied fears. This woman though, is as unreadable and as ungovernable as a wild cat and I tell you, I live in absolute terror of her most of the time. My life is on fire here.'

He continued to say that he was not planning to return to college. He wrote that he found it utterly sterile compared with the influence now at work on him. He hastened to add that the poet was not his only source of guidance, but that his 'guvnor' was showing him a pleasure in the countryside that he had never believed possible. He told me that he now adored the smell of earth and even the sting of a wasp could seem pleasant to him. City life would be unbearable and its rewards could only be nil after the lessons of the summer.

The letter finished: 'I have the cash now to come with you to Venice, but no longer the will. I would shrivel there away from this estate. Money is of no consequence to me now. I trust it never will be again. Look,' he wrote, 'take what money I have by me. I'll not need it here.'

He sent me £150, a great deal in those days, and I am ashamed to say I accepted it – all in dirty five pound notes that I knew he had grubbed from the potato field – and spent it all along the shores of the Adriatic. The money was never mentioned between us again. To him it was as though it had never existed: with me, it always weighed sorely on my conscience. I felt that he was advancing along strange paths without me: I was left behind and I had grasped at the earthly and the humdrum with the ugliest of greed. I suppose to be truthful, I never really forgave him for his generosity.

Chapter VIII

The weeks progressed; it was one of the very hot summers of that decade and the machine harvested so quickly on the dry soil that more and more often the day's work would finish by the late afternoon. Frequently, the old men were not even required and Joe had done his one hundred tons and more with just the women sorting above him. Life had opened out for him and the long evenings gave him time to see things before unknown to him.

Ian taught him many of the skills of the woods. Together, they searched the hedgerows for rabbits or helped the gamekeeper trace fox paths that wandered the length and breadth of the estate. They fished with the fly for the wild brown trout of the small river and enjoyed blissful late evening rises in the crystal chalk stream water. Tench fishing in the large lake; whistling up and feeding the pheasants in the drives; stalking the red deer deep in Mossymere; watching the owls in the barn by the Lengthsman's house; teaching the young gun dog correct manners; following the sparrowhawk to his nest in the pines around the deserted blacksmith's farm – the summer melted into Joe's memory for ever and left him a changed man.

Many dusks, Joe found himself near the Lengthsman's house in Mossymere. The old man worked the vegetable garden constantly in the evenings as the heat of the day faded and sometimes Maggie would be with him, despite her day's work on the harvester. But there were times when she would meet Joe and they would walk off together into the wood that she knew so well.

The early flirtations between the two people were well over. As the summer neared its end this was a deepening relationship. It bore an intensity that held them both locked, quite blind to the impossibility of their passion, oblivious to the dangers that threatened the obsession of theirs on every side. There came a period that marked them deeply: Joe's work on the machine was inevitably drawing to its end and the realisation that the mellowing, growing love was facing all manner of impossibilities left them both ravaged. They both wanted to have and hold in the continuing security of this one Mossymere summer and Joe was willing to give up anything to make this possible. They could not miss one night together now and when Maggie drew away to return to her sleeping house, the wrench in them both was a physical pain, real as any blow or cut to the quick. These last unions took place almost invariably in the ancient flint mines, the Devil's Dish to the southeast of Mossymere. The pit grew gloomy early and the dews never even quite dried away in the few hours that the sun's rays could penetrate to the bottom of the cavern. The moss there was a luxuriant bed and the elderflower hung over them like a roof. There they knew they would be alone in that place deeply feared by all on the estate. Maggie though, rejoiced in the Dish, midst the woodpeckers and the jays, amongst the ruins of the old foxes' earths. And when darkness fell, the bats came from crannies up and down the quarry-sides and flittered crazily after the night flies. So many of them the still air thrilled to their piping, to the rustling of their leather wings.

Joe talked of staying in the estate, of leaving college, of working full-time on the land. Maggie would tell him not to destroy his life. He grew more desperate as the days to the parting grew close and she equally had to beg him to leave, to go, even if not to forget her entirely, ever.

What Joe did not realise then, perhaps not ever, was that she was to suffer the most, that the parting would be always easier for him. She was a true love, yes, but he stood at an age of constant hope and optimism. He needed her today but he would soon be gone, never to forget, but always able to love again.

For her, the relationship was not more fundamental, but more essential and more desperate. Joe was Maggie's last chance at life. In such a place, she had always had so little choice. Failing Ian, then the Lengthsman was always bound to be her lot. How many men had she ever seen in her life? How many could she have seen even if she had ever wanted to? Joe's attentions had at first just been fun and flattery. The pace had, however, outstripped them both and had developed and grown out of all her proportions. Maggie always knew, even on those final summer nights that she could not leave the Lengthsman and Mossymere. They were too deeply ingrained in her life for that. But she could not bear to see Joe leave for with him went all her hope. She knew just how very little remained for her then. Middle age was close: old age and widowhood did not seem very much further off. She would know more poverty, not less, as her strengths declined and her earning power fell. She would know less fun and pleasure as her looks and vitality ebbed, lost and unadmired in the wood. All the nights Joe struggled to stay and she fought to make him leave, she realised she was surely pulling the curtains over her life, shutting out the last ray of light from her face. She accepted Joe physically at last, for she knew he would be her final memory.

'I must know that you really love me tonight,' Maggie once said to him. 'You can go and you will forget me. I accept all that as inevitable. But if you are deceiving me now, if all this is lies, if you don't feel for me as you say, then I really would kill you.' She shook her hair free of her shirt and tipped her face up into his. Her eyes widened slightly and she repeated, 'I would, love you as I do, I'd have to kill you if you were betraying me.'

And again Joe felt that with Maggie, he was dealing as with the most compelling and with the most ultimately dangerous of wild animals. His passion mingled with fear and it knew no bounds.

Chapter IX

At the very end of the harvest, the machine began to work long hours again. Joe's approaching departure was a factor and so was the estate's desire to complete the last remaining acres and move Ian and the focus of the work on to the true autumnal tasks of ploughing and planting. The thousand tons of potatoes remaining needed to be raised in a week and the whole gang sweated under a near impossible task. Now Maggie worked right through: there was no old man who could cope with the torrent of potatoes off the belt into Joe's sacks. Dusk was falling earlier and the canvas awning was lit brilliantly by lanterns that reflected off the dew-soaked potato leaves just as the ships' lights might have danced off the waves of the sea.

On board, everyone was always tired. The old men's complaints grumbled on.

'A drink? The pub's shut old partner! Get your head down! Get to it, you old buggers! What's the good of a belly full of beer to men like you? Make your penny now, whiles you can!' This was Ian's way to grind the potatoes from the earth to the very last one. But Maggie was up there with the old men and she talked and told them tales to while away the hours the potato rows slowly went down before them. She made them smile, she made them laugh and some nights, in the end, she made them sing as the moon rose up through Mossymere.

It was a growing moon all that week and this last night,

Maggie doused the lamps and they found they could work almost as quickly as in the daylight. At the summer's start, Joe would have merely mouthed the words of her songs, but now he sang with confidence and a youthfulness and a freshness that stood proud from the grumbleweed notes of the ancient men. A stranger, looking on from the wood or the track, would have mistaken the scene for a wild, bizarre party. He would never have guessed the tiredness or the desperation the gay words were drawn out to mask. The last night of all. Not long before midnight. Two rows of potatoes remained, one to the track and the other back into the wood's shadow.

Lordie stood a grey figure urging Ian on. The success of the crop and of the estate's farming was all to Lordie. Rather like Ian himself, he could not leave a job: he could not sleep easy, until he knew the best possible had been done for his beloved land. Though he was hard, all knew he was fair and that he felt for the soil in a way the countryman understood. There were no complaints of him: the crop would be finished that night and the whole gang knew it.

The last night. The last row and Joe, in exhaustion, had to pause. For the final furlong, Maggie, a second time, took his place on the boards.

'Soft bugger,' an old voice said from the shadows, lost as the riddles began to work again. And that was how the summer's work ended: Maggie's little body, strong nearly as Joe's but with a grace few men possessed, never losing balance as the platform bucked over the very last of the rutted soil. The end of the final row: the wood loomed: the potatoes worked their way through the machine and the very last of the year's crop fell into Maggie's sack. Half a cheer rose up from the old men and they made off for their bicycles. Satisfied, Lordie disappeared into the night.

'That'll do damn it. Leave the machine for me tomorrow,' said Ian. Joe and Maggie were alone.

Chapter X

Neither went home.

Towards the dawn the silence of the wood around the shed was broken. Joe swung back the door and lifted his head from the nest of potato sacks and coats that surrounded them both. The new light fell over Maggie, still asleep next to him. Joe watched carefully: there was mist in the wood and over the lowes of the field and to see anything clearly was not possible. A branch though cracked and damp bracken unmistakably swathed back. Now Joe stirred fully and crept towards the door, half in fear of the Lengthsman, of the man who never slept coming at them through the gloom, this man who knew the forest so that he could step as quietly as a rabbit through it. A man who knew all its paths, even how the nettles or the loosestrife should hang and who could recognise a bramble shoot bruised by the foot of a stranger or an intruder. He had eyesight like the sparrowhawk and hearing like the red deer. Joe feared the sharpness of this fox coming in on its prey.

Enough minutes passed to let the light grow a little stronger and Joe became aware of shapes on the fringe of the field and the wood. In streaks, grey was painted on grey. Columns of this greyness drifted to surround the lovers' hut. They moved slowly, wary, images of pewter from the still carved wood. Then, a stag cleared the single strand fence and stood only yards from Joe's gaze; so close to see his intelligent brown eyes scan the scene, to feel his cough, to shake from his roar that called the hinds into the field to feed. Around and around the hut the herd ate. They picked all the potatoes left from the last, hurried, moonlit rows: they muzzled over those sacks left untied and each of the dozen animals gorged in the cold air as their breath clouded over them and faded them into a still deeper mist.

The chill of air had awoken Maggie as she too lay watching, on this, Joe's last day on the estate. Eventually, the rising sun drew the vapours further out of the moist woodland until the whole field was sheeted in lemon flame with the stag a deep-throated silhouette in its centre. A sudden movement brushed a spade. It knocked the door. It fell on to the earth outside and though Joe's eyes had never wavered, the field was now deserted, as if the herd had never been there, as if the overturned sacks were only the old man's carelessness, as if the herd's whole presence had been a mere trick of light half formed, a play of the imagination, a fantasy and nothing more. Not even the dry soil took any imprint of the half hundred hooves. Nothing. A memory only of beauty.

'Where will you be tonight?' Maggie asked.

'A place I now hate. Some hundreds of miles from a place I now love,' Joe replied.

'The time has come then,' Maggie said. 'I feel as if I had waited a thousand years for you and all those empty days were forgotten when you arrived and, oh my God, how I'll miss you now you're gone.'

Neither could let go. As the sun rose higher still, over the watching trees of Mossymere, they made love again with the saddest of joy. They washed in the stream that flanked the wood. They tidied the shed and when it came to it, Joe even walked the field to kiss the harvester farewell. He whispered to it how he knew life on the boards had changed him.

Maggie began to walk home and told Joe to leave her

there at the hut. He refused and they held hands tightly around the field, through the oak grove until they reached the Devil's Dish. From there, they could see smoke from the Mossymere cottage chimney and hear a door close sharply. The Lengthsman was about.

'How will you explain this?' Joe asked.

'I don't know, darling, I don't care.'

'Will he ask?'

'I doubt it. He doesn't need. He's known me over thirty, no nearly forty years, and I haven't been able to hide you from him. Perhaps he hasn't even minded. I don't know. I just don't know anymore,' she ended, quietly.

'Maggie, can't you tell me now at least why you are with him, what you are doing here? You know I love you and there's nothing you'd ever need to hide.'

'Oh, that's not it at all,' she broke in. 'I've never told you because it's private, buried history, and all history has ever done is to disturb the calm of the present. I'll tell you now though, if you want to understand why in minutes I'll go along that avenue, back to him, why I do love him in a real way, why I'll always feel tenderness towards him. I know Ian told you how he brought me up – I've explained you that much myself. What few people know is that he actually saved my life. He really did, from a death at the place we now stand. You see, we are both tied up, me, him, here. It was wrong of you to come. It was worse that I even thought of wanting to escape with you.'

Chapter XI

It was autumn when Joe read me a letter that he had received days earlier. I had seen him study it over and over in the lights of dying afternoons, framed in the window of our room at college. The gaunt trees of the common behind him, the drab city lights beginning to glow.

'Listen. This was my summer. You've asked enough and I've said nothing, so perhaps you deserve to hear this. It's from someone who is the dearest to me in the world.' He picked up the letter and cleared his throat. He read all the time with his back towards me, the last of the November light aglow around him.

'I thought about the last time we made love, that night there was a full moon to peep at us and paint you silver. It seemed like a lifetime that you were mine and there was no one to deny that we were together. So happy together weren't we? I, at least, felt how it is to be adored. Oh, my lovely, lovely man, nothing you could ever do could be less than perfect. You are my god. Every breath, every kiss, every touch is a kind of magic. I love your hair, I love your body, how it smelled of sunshine, of the dust of the field, of the green damp of the Dish here. Remember that? I loved your hands so brown that in the moonbeams they looked like ebony. Ivory your eyes. Gold-dust breath. There's beauty in every last inch of you. Darling man.

'And how am I going to live without you, now that you've

gone? I envy you sleeping alone tonight when all I want is to lie watching the night gradually lighten, thinking of you – not to be touched by another, not to hear another breath, not to allow any other person into our world. You are gone. I fear you will never come back. I will live and die in this place without you and every night of my life I will remember. Every night, after midnight, I will sit up, open my eyes and say a prayer that you will return, that you and I can be forever together like we were that very last time. I'd ask you again not to betray me, even though you are hundreds of miles away. You will not return to a place where I can have hold of you again. How do I sign this letter? Love is true? Yours to the grave is true? I will never forget you and if you were to return to Mossymere, you would find me waiting, I promise you that. You said you would ring me. I cannot forget that, my darling, because how soon you forget that I am not even on the telephone.' When Joe stopped, there was a long silence between us.

Then he told me all. 'That was my summer,' he said. 'I will go back. Whatever happens, I will go back to her.'

'Let it go, Joe,' I'd wanted to say. 'Let it be – a butterfly, let it fly by.' I could not say anything. Nor could he. Though he never referred to that summer again – not for two decades – I knew he never forgot it, never escaped, always laboured under it, like a spell.

'Beware this is not just nostalgia,' I risked saying at the end of term, when we were blacktied and more than half drunk.

'A good point,' he conceded. 'But as wrong as you have ever been. As stupidly unseeing as you'll always be. I'll always be there. I am now. This has been the one peak of perfection in my entire life and I'll never, ever deny it.' Mossymere was never mentioned again in our youth.

Whether it was because Joe was older, stronger, or more talented than I, his words then and his reaction to the letter in the future affected me greatly. He had returned from Mossymere changed: a man with a past. I don't wish to place too much stress on that far-off, whimsical term of ours, but Joe's passion, his inner agony could be the reason I personally never married. Rather, it has been my first maxim that whenever I have felt in love, I have booked on to the next plane. I have always been destined to look on at the affairs of others, always afraid to make myself vulnerable in the way Joe was then, and was to be again in the future. In this respect I am a coward. I have never known the type of joy that Joe found in Mossymere – but I have never been tinged by the despair either. My life has been the easier of the two. I believe I have kept things much better in their right place.

Part Three

The Keeper

Chapter I

I relay as far as I can everything that Joe told me that particular afternoon about Maggie's birth. I am sure that he recounted the story as precisely as it was possible to remember it. Equally, he believed her account to be as accurate as she could make from what she herself was told. I, therefore, pass this on at third, no, at fourth hand and I cannot say if history can withstand so many interpretations and remain faithful. I can make no guarantees and yet perhaps this has been less distorted than the more recent passages that have been more coloured by violent emotions. There were certain things at the time of the telling that I wanted to ask Joe. For example, the Smith of the tale falls in love with the Keeper's wife on only an initial sighting. He, the Smith, was a man of substance and why this rock of a man should be so attracted so quickly I was not told. Perhaps the chemistry of love is so strong that no one before found the question worth the asking. Certainly at this distance in time, the man's vulnerability I find strange, even to a previously unknown fragility and an uncommon loveliness. History, though, is decorated with the unexpected: this gives it charm, interest and an illogicality that even a man of reason has to live with, to accept and in the end, come to find attractive. I said I know the story so well and yet there are so many aspects even I find so disturbing and unexpected.

I can say that the Keeper and his child bride were the first people to inhabit the repaired Mossymere house, and the first to live on the site as more than passing wanderers for many centuries. It was high summer when they arrived and the season glowed on both of them with all the golds and greens of the huge woodland. Their first weeks were ones of glorious weather: there were nights of heavy dews verging on frosts, of star spangled skies, days of heady winds and the heavens east to west of brightest blue. Peewits cried over the surrounding fields in the darkness and all the while the swallows began to gather from off the rivers and the meres soon to slip off south in their travelling caravans.

The times were busy for these newcomers to the forest. The Keeper put up his dog runs, a shelter for the horse and walked Mossymere by day and night, searching, marking trees, and planning drives and avenues for the shooting parties that were to come. He was well aware of the foxes, only a fool would not be, and was equally confident that he would be their master. Journey after journey, he noted their runs and their earths and planned his battles against them when he would fall like a hammer from the skies. All this was the character of the Keeper, for, though he was young, he was determined and it was fiercely in his nature to do well. His mission was to make the shoot talked about the county over and force the other estates, where he had always been underkeeper, to wish they had never let him go.

This rough ambition had impressed Lordie when the two had met at the Swancoots estate office.

'Give me the chance, sir,' the tall blonde Keeper had said, 'and you'll never regret it. If I can't make this shoot work then no one will. I'll tell you sir, give me the job and I'll work and work at it till I drop.'

'The place is a lonely one,' Lordie had said, 'and I know the house won't be too homely for a man on his own. A wife,

I would have thought, would be a comfort and of great use out there.'

'I'll see to that at once, sir, that is supposing you are kind enough to give me the chance. There's someone I knows who'll do me right enough and will jump at the thought of being a Keeper's wife.' Lordie liked this man's confidence and his obvious desire to get things done. He marked his vivid blue eyes, so very piercing, that looked neither right nor left, but direct into his own. He believed that the Keeper was his type of man, straight, hardworking but not someone to cross. His references had made that plain. His previous employers had found him to be a chap of spirit, fire even, who didn't always know when to hold his peace and to be silent, or even accept advice when well meant and expertly given. Still, Lordie reckoned, the keeper had made his mistakes in the past, at other people's expense, and he was willing to give him the opportunity. The whole situation at Mossymere demanded a man of exceptional quality, which for good or ill, the young man in front of him quite obviously possessed.

'A wife, sir, yes of course! I'd thought of that one meself.'

There was a young girl two days' travel or more away in his native village who was afraid of losing him and equally afraid of accepting him. She nodded her lovely head when asked a week later and now found herself mistress of Mossymere, though hardly more than a girl from school. She took to the wood fretfully, like a songbird in a new cage, she was happy in the sunlight and frightened in the emergent shadows. Her heart skipped at the cry of an owl or the lurch of an oak in the wind and she slipped from dream into nightmare and back again every bit as quickly as a cloud over the face of the moon. Her new husband alarmed her, she was frightened of his intensity, his deep silence and the fire that burned so privately inside him that she felt barred from even the warming of her hands. He was no man for pleasantries and had been a near stranger to her before the marriage as he was now in all his constant comings and goings. Sometimes, she knew his warm body in the small hours, but still a cold, deserted bed by dawn. Other times, she tried to find him in the woodland, only to lose herself in the endless lookalike green acres. If she stayed alone in the cottage, then the wall clock echoed in her head and she cried with memories of her lost family, friends and village. And all the while, the pace of the sun sinking quickly towards autumn disturbed and depressed her. Weeks into her Mossymere existence she had seen hardly a soul but for the Keeper's back in the moonbeams or his light jinking off through the wood as he dug in his traps and his snares. Memories of old laughter never left her for long and her eyes misted over at the times lost and the spartan world come so suddenly to her young life.

'Mother,' she wanted to say. 'Come and fetch me and take me home and save me from this dreadful place and this strange man that I do not understand.' Instead, she wrote that life was quite fine and that she sent her love to all and she hoped they would meet sometime in the year following.

CHAPTER II

The house nearest to the Mossymere cottage belonged to the Smith. He had come to the estate a young man and soon prospered through hard work and avoidance of women, of drinking and of anything that could be classed as a distraction. He was a tower of strength to all, seen as an honest dealer, exceptionally quiet and thoughtful and yet never one to make a real friend. Rather he enjoyed being alone: the lamp at his forge burned well into the night as he worked happily in isolation, in his private world. He was a byword for industry. He never minded being called out, not on a Sunday, not late at night, if a horse's shoe had gone and there was work for it waiting to be done. The other blessing was his way with the animals. As his hands brushed their legs and tapped their knees, then every horse would cock up his hoof and stand patiently until the job was done. He was a wonder that one, and in demand from the world well outside the estate. In all it was no surprise when he was able to build his own house on land bought from the estate.

The site he chose was well away from any other houses and the building crowned a hill's crest, overlooking the valley, halfway exactly between the village and Mossymere. He had not been at all pleased when the renovations had begun on the Keeper's house, for even though a near mile away, he still saw it as an intrusion on the privacy he loved and he kept well away from the first weeks of the Keeper's occupation. Towards the end of the good weather, however, the Smith had been working outside the estate and had taken the track through the forest homewards. It was the late afternoon when he passed the Mossymere house and a golden light from across the field lit up that side of the building not shielded by the wood and dusted it with angeldown and magic.

He paused and in an upper window saw the young girl framed for an instant as she looked out over the world for sight of company or any human kind. My history cannot tell if she were really beautiful or for just that second, or if her loneliness and the blazing light combined to charm him, but the Smith found all he wanted in the world when he looked at her. The track ahead sparkled, the cottage was a castle, the girl was a princess and the Smith lost his heart in the time it takes the sun to fall an eyelash through the sky.

She herself could not have been aware of him, black waistcoated, melted into one with the falling shadows from the oak trees and so he could watch her like a shepherd views a planet above, alone and aloof from the world. Time passed and as the sun dropped, mists rolled in over the fields and it became quickly cold. The Keeper's wife lit a candle and as the flame grew it must have made her seem all the more fragile, more desirable, as it flickered in her eyes, running over her lips, tracing her cheek bones and flecking the blonde in her hair. Only as true darkness fell, did the Smith leave the oak hedge and move to the garden fence, hanging in the shadow of an old crab apple tree. From there he saw her breath mist on the glass and her child's finger draw patterns in it. When the Keeper's bicycle swung into the lane the Smith departed, drawing away gently into the countryside, shadow into shadow, heartbeat into heartbeat.

The track to his home exists still, narrow, sanded, steep in parts and of course not another dwelling on the way. Not a light, not a sound, not a soul rippled her image in his mind.

He took his supper alone in the large house and went up to the great bedroom that overlooked the village. For a moment he watched the few lights shining there and then walked purposefully into the bedroom that gave out north. The window was small and set so high in the wall that even the tall Smith needed to bring up a trunk to see to the wood through it. For seconds he watched until a sigh of wind lifted a branch somewhere and a distant light glowed. Then the Smith jumped down and set to his great iron bed with a spanner. Piece by piece he dragged it along the landing and into the smaller room. He gouged the fresh pine, he sweated and he shoved, but he did not think of rest until the job was done. Early next morning he stood on the bed and watched the wood until he saw smoke curl from the Keeper's chimney from the fire his new beloved had made. Then he lay half an hour more in the warmth of the sheets, through the slow autumn dawn, thinking of her, of her slight shoulders, of her lips parted as they had been, slightly, as though in miraculous prayer.

Chapter III

The weather broke: from beauty it became beast overnight with continuing storms and rains. In the hastily built cottage, the defects soon showed themselves and the lifting tiles, the overflowing drains, the cracked chimney stack, the swelling doors and the damp in all the floors and walls ruined every attempt the young girl had made to create a home there. Outside, the woods became a misery to work in. Tracks were less easy to follow, scents were washed away in an hour of rain and the dead bracken folded and rotted in a brown morass. The cleansing breezes of the fine weather dropped quite away and now the rain fell vertically through the all but still air. In the wood, a raindrop could be heard, or a falling leaf, a creak of the Keeper's boots, or the snap of a setting trap and even the click of the 12 bore's hammer. Though he had shot, poisoned or trapped many foxes, the Keeper's tally now fell again as the animals grew wise to his tricks. The carcasses on his line grew old, stale and blown and few of their fellows followed them, even though the onset of the winter brought more foxes into Mossymere.

Such had been their habit since misted times and no keeper could stop them searching out the warmth of the deep sand earths, sheltered from the cold north-easterlies by the oakwoods. From all over the estate and from beyond its borders, the animals drew in towards the forest. They followed old routes, at night, crossing parishes, farms, the river and its streams and there was nothing that the Keeper could do to stop them but to spend even longer hours in the wood, searching, plotting and worrying about his future in the job that he ever feared to be getting beyond him.

A very large dog fox had come lately to Mossymere. The creature was in his prime, alert, resourceful and an inch or probably two or three, longer and taller than any other in the wood. His coat also was particularly fine, the deepest of russet red and his muzzle shapely, rather broad with intelligence that blazed from the pale eyes. The fox had had his brushes with men and he hated them. In his eight years of life, he had lost two of his vixens to Keeper's lines outside the estate and had come to find his third in Mossymere. Presuming knowledge is impossible to deny in a fox and the presence of this new Keeper did not please him.

The Keeper was first alerted by the abnormal size of his prints on a soft headland and then, a while afterwards, he had seen the animal a second travelling on an avenue at dusk. The two of them had met at only ten yards and the fox had seemed to recognise and accept its fate. He had stopped and sat on the moss carpet as the Keeper raised his gun, took aim and squeezed the trigger. It jammed. There was a metallic rasp and nothing more. But for that trick of fate, for the fluke of engineering that had never occurred before, the whole story of Mossymere might well have been stillborn. An escaped fox, taken out of context, should have meant little. As the history of Mossymere developed, however, the episode was soon to prove central. The fox rippled like a breeze through the darkening trees and the Keeper stood soaked by the rain for near on an hour. The cold that he had been carrying for days became a fever which racked him in spasms of coughing and pain. His face had paled and his eyes burned with illness and with rage and he shuffled back through the avenue to take to his bed and lie there a full four days.

Ill though he was, and his sleep often became delirious, he could still recognise the voice of the Smith in the room beneath, or hear his wife's bicycle on the track at dusk as she pedalled off to who knows where but away from that dark house and all its gloom.

From the very beginning the Smith had found it easy to call at the Keeper's house. As a neighbour and a tradesman he had every excuse and he presented himself formally the next day as one who might be needed as the winter closed in and the snow falls blanketed the wood off from all other contact. But to speak to the girl of all the things in his mind he, of course, found impossible. Though his heart burst and his hands shook when he held his teacup, all he could do was ask permission to come again. When he left, the impression he took with him was as cherished and as lovely seen close as the vision at the candlelit window.

He dreamed of the open eyes that danced, of the blonde hair and clear skin and the voice so soft and warm with its lilt of ever present, stifled laughter. Then he called again. Did his dog's barking trouble her at night, when it heard the vixen's cry? No, not at all. She was glad to hear it, poor thing, and comforted to know the presence of company down the track when the Keeper was gone so long. Would she like any special shopping done when he had to visit the market town next? Yes she would and she would prepare a list. Thank you for calling. And for listening like he did when she spoke of her past, of her family, of her husband, of her hopes and fears, her whims and her fancies. She began, as the days and visits passed, to wait for him like a love-starved kitten, to laugh more and more at his stories and positively squirm again for his presence. Only once in all that time did the Keeper return to find the Smith there and then the conversation quickly waned and the visitor had gone on his way.

Left alone by Keeper and Smith both, the night pulled in

on her; the image of the Smith lengthened; his imprint left heavily on the chair; the scuff of his boots muddied on the rug by the door; a whisker of his beard on the rim of a cup where the sugar had glued it fast. She could recognize his thumbprint beneath her eye, stamping the fledgling cheekbone as his own. A hundred times, she looked in the mirror at the rose blooming on her neck which burned and grew where his white teeth had ripped and closed in passion and play.

Close her eyes a second – dare she – and the brown, broad arm was around her again and the smile was dancing in his eyes. Hold her breath, sigh deeply and the joy between them relit the darkness, overlapped the room, become her gaol.

She cried that her world could be so upset: that her husband could be a stranger: that a stranger could be her welcomed lover and that she had never once struggled to keep her virtue, her horizons, in any focus. Just how the quake of the earth had erupted she could not know, but accept it she must, or die desolate, emotion muzzled in Mossymere before her natural time was through.

'Mother,' again she longed to write, 'tell me, tell me please, what should I do ...'

Once, in his illness, the Keeper had struggled to the window of his room and seen his wife's slight figure over the handlebars, working to keep the bicycle upright on the sodden sand track. Her clothes clung to her slim body and the constant rain streaked the pane as he hammered on it and called out her name. But she was gone, he slept again and his dreams were wild. He screamed out loud at the dog fox that he could sense digging at the foundations of the cottage, at the innards of his very heart. The fox was scuffling at the doors, growling at the dogs, baring its teeth in a wolfish red snarl. The animal's coat was blooded, stuck with feathers, and now he was rolling in the straw of the woodland rides and pacing the pheasant runs. The Keeper could smell the fox's urine on the sheets and feel the sour breath pant at his cheeks and brow. And always, always the animal was barking, howling, both day and night through his mind, racking his body.

Some time later, the Keeper saw his wife's child's breasts under the Smith's rough hand, a tongue that slipped so wantonly around her mouth and over her throat and belly and he cried again when he saw that the strong pink tongue that now slipped between his wife's opening legs slid from the mask of a fox. His wife's eyes stared into his sleep, wide with pleasure, reflecting the moon, the Smith's bearded head and the animal there, on his haunches, grinning at all he saw. The Keeper was in constant bodily pain and he felt his shoulders ache when the lord of the estate had shaken him and called, 'The foxes man! The foxes man! What are you doing about the foxes? Do you hear? The foxes!'

The day dawned that the room began to move more slowly around him and shuddered giddily to a stop. His head no longer burned and his eyes became more placid. He could sit up, then eat, soon walk and finally, though weak, he knew he was sound enough to face the winter wood once more. His illness had, however, left its scars deep in him somewhere, on his soul, perhaps in his spirit. His nightmares cast something of horror into his reality and they never fully receded, but left their shadows on him. The storm had broken around him and had burst his life wide open that winter and though his body sharpened, he was more and more a ruined man. To catch the big dog fox became the Keeper's obsession. He saw the animal now as the maggot in his soul and the cancer of his luck and the foundation of all the threats of his existence. He had become man in the clutches of doom, quite helpless before the bad weather, a victim of the short days and the wind-whipped leaves, an inhabitant of a lonely world which he had created utterly without joy.

His now near solitary existence took on this single purpose and through the cold days and bitter nights of the back of the year he trudged the wood, killing and maiming all vermin as he went. His poison killed the barn owl that had eaten a contaminated shrew and failed even to return home to die. It fell on an avenue and its features moved softly in the wind, a life of their own. A Lengthsman, a road mender today, came across the bird and lifted it high above him. The light caught the browns of the bird's feathers and kindled them to flame: the whites were of shades even more brilliant and now the winged wizard face was cold and small in his rough hands. The Lengthsman cursed the waste and with the shovel from his back, he buried the bird in the frosted ground.

Chapter IV

The girl said to the Smith that she was ever more frightened, it was as if the bones plastered up in the walls of the cottage were beginning to talk to her. They called out to her as she slept, tales of murder, woe and despair. She recalled a cub or a kitten, attacked by a snake and its mouth open wide in silent screams, so piercing that they shook her awake. The long nights were a misery for her, lying from the early hours, her ears pricked for the dropping of a latch or the sound of shuffling footsteps. She said that she was terrified and that she could not live there in the cottage much longer. The Keeper and she had become virtual strangers: she never knew if he were in the house, dozing in the chair, warmed by the embers of the previous day's fire, or if he were out somewhere in the wind and the blow, either searching or sheltering rough in a barn or a shed. The darkness was endless for her she told the Smith, as she paced her room, praying for the shabby dawn light and an end to the voices of the past. When she did sleep, the piercing cold gnawed her and she awoke little refreshed, still grey and drawn.

'Never you mind,' the Smith had told her. 'I regard you as my wife now and if you'll have me, we'll be gone from all this, the estate, him and everyone. We can leave just as ever you wish it.' In his steady way, the Smith had made his plans for their desertion whenever that day should come. The Smith now was deeply in love, but he had recovered his old poise and his strength of purpose. He was the man again that he had always been, capable and caring, but now he had taken on this added responsibility.

The Lengthsman had also spoken to the Smith. He had overheard fierce arguments from time to time as he trudged the pathways through Mossymere. He had witnessed a blow when he was working on the track near the Smith's house on the hill. The girl had been on her bicycle, in the late afternoon, returning into the wood when from the trees the Keeper had run out, stopped her and pulled her roughly from the saddle. He had swung the butt of his gun at her cheek and had left her there where she fell for the Lengthsman himself to bring around and escort home. How the Lengthsman had kept his own patience he had not known. His impulse had been to chase into the woodland, pull the Keeper down, wrest away his gun and batter him with the pick at his shoulder. There was a violence in the Lengthsman that bubbled and seethed and he had kept in check only for the sake of the girl.

Days were still short, the period of storm set in and all the tracks became impassable in the drifting snow that fell night after night from cygnet-down skies. Even at noon the light in the small-windowed rooms was bottle green and so weak that it quickly faded into almost perpetual twilight. The Keeper dare not leave the walls but sulked before his gun and his traps, eating only little, speaking not at all and sleeping the bulk of his time out. Silence was within and without: all was quiet under the immense white blanket. Unspoken suspicion and fresh menace and dread came down with each succeeding snowfall and the drifts between man and wife became utterly impassable. She lived exclusively in her own bedroom and he downstairs or in the yard or the stables so that there could never be the chance of a forgiving glance or of a forgetful smile. The ruinous days of the cottage's past seemed to speak once more in the girl's pale face and wide yearning eyes and her cough that rang in the petrified air, off the stark walls, was a sound that the centuries of dispossessed would have recognised in that place. And the Keeper, winding his way through the snow sheet could have been just another refugee from the past.

Once in that spell of cruel weather the Smith struggled through to Mossymere as the dusk began to fall. He abandoned the track which lay waist deep in drifts and took off northwards over the ploughed field where the gales had scraped away the bulk of the snow and the frost had frozen the soil under his boot. A lamp burned from the young wife's window and the Smith approached it to call up softly her name. He saw first her shadow and then her face above him as she tried to force open the iced window frame. All was in vain. For a minute, more, they conducted silent, desperate conversation and then, love was not enough. A gun crackled the stillness from an outbuilding and shot spattered into the snowladen bushes around. The Smith hesitated, roared defiance, but respecting the girl's signs, he slipped away into the fast enveloping darkness. And she cried most of the remaining night, long and cold enough to freeze her tears where they fell.

CHAPTER V

One night there was no frost, nor was there the next, even though it was close on a full moon and the stars danced in a cloudless sky. The sun of the next day felt warm and the following evening the lapwings began to call from the fields on the verge of Mossymere. Their peewit calls attracted the Keeper's wife to them, to watch as they hovered and tumbled, silhouettes against the bright sky or fell as shadows on the earth. The girl listened until nearly midnight and then went along the track a little way into the meadow to be even closer. She leaned against the gate there, looked up into the immense silken sky and was so still that the birds came back once more and wheeled around her so close, as if to skim her hair.

The Lengthsman passing by the wood saw the girl's outline and stopped. 'Are you not cold?' he asked tenderly, seeing she was without any coat.

'No,' she said, 'I'm just watching the birds here.'

'Ah, the peewits. They're a grand sight they are. Night long they'll be a-singing and a-courting here. Love can be a deal of fun, it seems, if you don't let it get to you.' The girl cradled her swollen stomach quite visible in the moonlight.

'What will you call it?' he asked pointing at her. She looked up and around and said, 'Peewit, I think!'

'Ay. That would be a fine name for a little man born in such a place. But supposing it's a girl, then Peewit wouldn't really do for her.' The girl became pensive and the Lengthsman looked up at the sky where a bird twisted close to them. Its feathers flashed with the reflected glory of the moon and gleamed brilliantly like a shield. Or a shell.

'That's like a pearl I'd say,' the Lengthsman muttered. 'The name Margaret mean pearl don't it? I remember hearing that once.'

'I don't know about that. It could do. I'm sure you're right, but I don't like the full name a lot. Maggie, Maggie though is all right. Yes. I do like Maggie.'

'That's easily decided then,' the Lengthsman concluded. 'Peewit for a boy and Maggie for a girl then.'

They were quiet a long time and then the girl asked, 'If anything should happen to us, to me I mean, would you possibly do something to look after it?'

'Nothing will happen,' the Lengthsman said, 'but, yes, of course I would, my dear woman. Of course.' A bond had grown between the two since the Keeper's attack in the wood and the Lengthsman, though wild when aroused, was more often gentle and protective to any being that was in need. 'I would treat any child of yours just as tenderly as if it were my own flesh and blood,' he said. 'Count on it, girl. You can depend on me, you know.'

There followed the occasional miracle days of snowdrop time when the warming sun lured the flies from the cracked barn walls. Bluebells, primroses, whirls of lilac and then the first cuckoo called. There followed bees in the blossom, harebells in the cascades and the shepherd was lambing every night. The girl grew even heavier and her walks with the Smith became more and more slow. They held hands openly now and he stopped in fascination with her little finger lifting it from the rest, comparing it with his own, like an island beside a whole continent.

'Could it be mine?' the Smith asked finally one day.

'It could be yours,' the Keeper's wife answered carefully.

They wandered on a pace and sat under a tree of cherry blossom.

'Well, is it mine?' he tried again. 'Do you think it is anyways?' The girl said nothing. 'I'd like to think it was mine, you know,' he said. She looked straight at him now. 'Really I would.' He saw the trace of a smile on her lips. 'I'd really love it if you says the little blighter was mine.' The girl began to laugh and she threw back her veil of blonde hair. She seized him by the beard and pulled him down to kiss.

'Of course it's yours, you fool. I've never done nothing with him. Not since the first days we've been here and that's well over the time. I'd reckon it was that first visit of mine to your house but I'd never say nothing for fear of losing you. I always knew though that whatever happened, boy or girl, it will be strong like you and well worth having and I'd love you both very much.' The Smith whooped with joy. He seized his hat from his head, whirled it in the air and threw it far back into the forest.

'I've never heard nothing sweeter than that in my life,' he bubbled. 'Now that's sorted out between us, we can act. We can look now, positive like, to the future.'

The Keeper meanwhile was away after the dog fox that had taken a mate and he had pledged his soul to find out where. He combed Foxburrows, the first time that it had been disturbed in breeding time, and he created havoc there. He lived away from the cottage now and barely went back but for clothes, food and trapping gear. He slept rough and went about like a tramp. He was an object of fear in the estate. His hair grew long, unkempt and unwashed, and his moleskins were tattered and grimed with dirt and blood. Village boys dared not even approach the wood - they said they could even smell him on the wind - and it was not unusual for him to shoot over the heads of any stranger that he saw. Word got back to Swancoots that the man was deranged, dangerous and running amok in Mossymere.

As the only man who knew where to find the Keeper day to day in the big wood, the Lengthsman took on a role of go-between. He could follow the Keeper's tracks and the occasional sound of gunshot and he ran him down first in the new plantation, eating by a fire. The two men were very distant – the job was quite distasteful to the Lengthsman. He could hardly bear to look at the Keeper and would remain standing in his presence. At the slightest word open fighting could have broken out between them.

'You'd better know that your wife is in labour early. The infant will likely die and the mother might well too. I've looked for ye a day or more to tell you this.'

'Well then, thank you, but I don't know what business it is of yours.'

'Neighbourly concern is all. In a place like this we must all help each other out.' The Keeper shrugged.

'As you say. I thank you again and I'll be home when I can. The girl is a strong 'un and she don't need me to fuss around her when there's work to be done.' Even when the baby was born, and when both lived, the Keeper rarely returned to the house. It was as if he knew that the child was no concern of his.

Chapter VI

It was four in the morning and the Keeper was on a path into Mossymere, coming from the south. He was tired and fretful. Though it was summer, his night had seemed a long one. Rain had fallen almost ceaselessly and he had tried to sleep in the shelter of an oak on the river hill, but had awoken both cold and damp. He drank some brandy to warm himself and lit a smoking fire, but he felt no better and decided on a rare day at thc cottage.

So it was that he was now stumbling home and once more fate took a giant hand, for, calling it a night also was the source of all his energy and passion, the dog fox. The animal, too, was down, depressed by the wind and rain and careless a single time. The strong breeze billowed the Keeper's scent away from the animal and so whirled the cornfield that the fox was crossing, that even his sight was affected. The animal reached a swathe of flattened grain and crossed it boldly, unthinkingly, rather than circumventing it to keep to the standing crop and remain hidden. One hundred yards away, the Keeper saw him, stopped and sank to his knees. He watched the animal through the field to the headland and then turn down into the deep bowels of the Devil's Dish itself. The Keeper sank on to the wet earth. His heart raced. His whole frame shook with cold violence. Never, never did the man believe the animal would build a lair so close to the cottage, to the home of his pursuer. Hate the creature though he always had, this final act of arrogance enraged him beyond all reason, so that any pleasure or gloating in the find was quite lost. He stumbled the few hundred yards to the cottage. All was quiet there. His wife and the child were sleeping in their own bedroom where the door was locked. Not that he tried it, but rather lay down fully clothed whilst his boots dropped on to the floorboards and his gun slipped from the soiled counterpane. He was asleep in seconds, a deep sleep, past hearing the birds busy in the growing light, or his wife moving on the landing, listening to his breathing at the keyhole and then cycling down the track, her baby strapped on behind her.

Mid-morning and the Keeper still slept and his snores were heard by the women at work in the field by the cottage. They looked up at his window and muttered together in fear and disgust both. When the Keeper did wake, he was hot in the sullen weather, felt more weary, not less and looked wild. He needed air and reached for the window. The frame had swollen in the winter's wet and the pane crashed noisily at his push. The glass shivered, broke, and fell out on to the pantiles. He saw the womens' faces turned up towards him and he pulled away, cut and cursing. Sultry weather and the harvest flies were in his hair, maddening him still further. He took his gun, his dog and cut past the women without a look on to the fields to the Dish. A buzzard marked the place, hanging high above the crater, kiting in the wind, pilot of the endless airwaves.

Chapter VII

The Keeper searched the rim of the Dish, carefully, meticulously even, but in vain. Yet he hardly expected to find the earth so near to the field and he moved down to a point ten yards into the pit and worked another circuit of the Dish's sides, through a tanglewood of bracken, nettle and bramble meshed beneath a bindweed lacing. Flies clouded him in their swarms and even his dog grew languid in the still heat and had to be beaten into further search. The Keeper was demented now, swearing under his breath, cursing the dog, kicking it when it slowed. Once, twice even he slipped, ripped his clothing on bramble and tore flesh on old flint scrapings in the ground. But there would be no let-up and round and round and down and down he hacked his way to the floor of the Dish. Here, he descended into a world of shade, lit by half light shafting through the towering screens of vegetation. No wind stirred there, not a breeze and the odours of the place lay heavy, of carrion, rotting, festering and growing in stench. Such was the pit of living nightmare so feared by the estate people. The pit, they believed, the Devil could well choose for his daytime grave, where he could scheme before launching venom into the world so beautiful above.

The earth of the dog fox was immense, a palace, tunnelled massively into the bowels of the Dish. The Keeper found three gateways to the mansion and the smell of fox hung thickly over each, and over the boneyard around. Birds, small mammals and fish even lay scattered around in whitened patterns of lost life. Quickly, the Keeper pulled his dog away and they climbed the wall of the Dish back into the day to find the sun well on its path down towards a tree line.

Back in his yard, the Keeper collected up a shovel, some traps, poison gas, his guns and then spent the hours till dusk pacing the lane alongside. He sat, but got to his feet once more. Rest he could not. His hands twisted when they were not thrust deep into the waistcoat pockets. His wrist still bled from the broken window and the pain of the flint cuts was a throbbing irritant to him. He smoked. He drank from a bottle and to the women working in the fields still he was like the genie from the dregs.

Eventually the skies cleared from the south and the west and a golden sunlight fell over the domain. The harvester's shadows lengthened and the fresher air grew still enough to hear a pigeon's wings clapping in the woods. The close, clammy day drifted away and now everything was bright and clean until even the dust smelled sweet. Coolness had driven away the flies and only spirals of midges hung in the avenues of trees. In a suddenly, seemingly perfect world one woman began to sing out from the field something of love and happiness that lifted the spirits of all around her. Her white bonnet and long skirts flowed as she danced to her own music around the sheaves of corn and the other working women. Her burst of joy though could not reach the Keeper, on the skyline, against the rim of the wood, defiant, a demon in his loneliness. The sky deepened into half light and new worlds began to shine and glitter in the cold, but he saw none of that. So still was the night that he heard his wife's bicycle from afar: so airless was it too that he could sense her breath, smell her hair, feel her heartbeat as she approached. Filled with anger, he gathered up his gear and left and all the young girl caught sight of was his broad back disappearing into the dusk. She watched him a long time until she was quite sure he had disappeared for the night and then she wheeled her bicycle and her baby in.

Chapter VIII

Just as the Keeper knew he would, the dog fox had left the Dish on the point of dusk to hunt food for his vixen and their three cubs that stayed around the earth, chasing tails and moths and shadows of the rising moon. Once tired, they went back into their labyrinth deep in the warm soil where all they heard was their heartbeats cradled in the noiseless sand. And so, as the Keeper had planned it all to be, their earth lay defenceless before him: the master had come to call at last.

He worked stealthily - and so quietly - in the gloom that hardly a tremor shook the soil above the fox family's heads. Into each of the openings the Keeper thrust the canisters of gas and at once shovelled the loose sand and dirt fast into all the cracks around. He then pulled up large timbers, the very ones the cubs had played around, and pressed them hard into the soft soil. The last fissures were pounded flat by blows of his spade and now the earth was a tomb, sealed entirely from air and light whilst the tide of gas seeped corridor by tunnel towards the imprisoned family. The Keeper finally set snares and traps all around the floor of the Dish, as many as he had, to catch the dog on his return towards the dawn. All done, he retreated back up the pit walls to sit on a stump, downwind of the earth, to nurse his gun and to await the final episode.

His look-out post was a half oak, slivered once in a storm,

which gave a view all over the Dish, virtually to the bottom even, across the bracken and over all the dog's possible entry routes. It also allowed him to peer through an avenue in the wood to his own cottage a short distance off, quite visible now that the wind had blown itself out through the stars and the trees were still. As he drank, he saw a light shine from the bedroom window, vivid in the darkness of the night. These were eerie times: blind beetles blundered into the bracken, the farm dog barked miles off and all the woodland creatures walked on tiptoes, keeping the silence, afraid to attract the Keeper's wrath and vengeance.

In the pit below, the poison had rolled to the tunnel's final turn and the cubs had nowhere else to crawl and escape. The vixen had picked them up and had pushed them along, but even she had used up all her alleys and this last one was blind and rebuffed them with a wall of damp sand. Go where she would, she would meet solid earth now, or the choking fumes. In vain did she claw at the funereal entrances and then in absolute despair at the endless soil that engulfed her. Her eyes misted, her dying cubs were shadows held out to absorb her, accompany her into the earth bound oblivion. The cubs she pulled under her and encompassed them with her paws. One of them tried to suckle, for comfort rather than food, and the others whimpered in ever quietening tones.

Shadows flickered on the windows of the Mossymere cottage: shadows that met and embraced and disappeared from the Keeper's view, leaving clear the bright mocking light once again. So two shadows merged and from the pit of the Keeper's being a rage began to mount. The Dish began to swim before his eyes: and then the stars like pixies called him and laughed, a twinkling laughter, soft laughter from space where all bodies rise and fall and where memories of love are never lost and forgotten, but live on eternally.

If there ever were a Devil in that Dish then he was abroad

now. The Keeper's shirt was unbuttoned: it lifted in a sudden breeze and slid off his shoulders. With it went the restraint of any normal man. He stood up, bare chested, and his heart pulsed with a hatred that exploded the night. He poisoned the earth and it had poisoned him. He fingered his gun. He tasted fox on the air and gagged on it. He smelled warm bedclothes and her opening her body to the shadows and the roar grew within him and burst out through the wood.

An animal now, a predator of the night, he leapt through the branches that lifted up to him and through the rides he loped on towards his prey. His scream had not been heard in the cottage, but had been by the dog hunting watervoles on the river a mile off. His orange eyes grew wide with an intelligence that spoke fear and his hackles rose. He scuffled up off his stomach and the red fox rippled homewards.

Chapter IX

The moon had risen full and the cottage stood in pools of shade and silver, silent in its clearing in the forest. The Keeper swayed on the verge of the trees, then, a crouching cat, he moved quickly towards the house. On that side lit by the moon, he tried the door which was locked. He followed the wall and tried each of the windows in turn but all were fastened. Twice he knocked at a swollen frame with its latch not fully down, but stopped afraid of waking the household inside. Now he was on the dark side of the building and stood a second in the mooncast shadow by the half-opened window of the back pantry. He lifted the hook noiselessly and his shape filled the room.

The baby lay asleep in the adjoining room, breathing softly in time with the wall clock. The Keeper bent over the cot and eased back the cover: the moon was bright there, flooded the infant's face and for minutes the Keeper hesitated. But there were boots not his own by the door to the stairwell and he fingered his gun. He opened a drawer and a knifeblade caught the silver light. So quiet, the door to the stairs opened, so gently he rocked on his feet and trod the first step and the second. The gun he cocked noiselessly and the dagger he lifted, poised for the hearts of those he sought. And his roar, his rage, the villagers claimed to hear from a mile away and for years later and certainly a foxy gentleman digging in the Devil's Dish cocked, for a moment, his ear.

They met there in the stairwell, the Keeper and the Smith, bodies tangled, fighting with every limb, tooth and nail, with hatred so immense each shed his own blood gladly for the taste of the other's. They tumbled the stairs into the room where the baby cried and where the moon glittered on their eyes, their sweat and the blood of both, each gashed by the hacking knife. Over the tiles they skidded and fought amongst the broken furniture and the dashed wall clock. The Smith's ear hung off loose into his beard and the stock of the gun smashed out the bridge of the Keeper's nose. They wrestled through the kitchen, rolled out into the yard and struggled in the earth of the garden patch. Their whole bodies flattened the nettle scrub, crushed the bracken and half pulled down the pheasant runs. In the dip there was shooting and the Keeper left the Smith there for dead.

Dragging himself back to the cottage, he kicked off the door that swung loose, and began to hunt the bedrooms, the cupboards, the chest and in the beds, the knife hanging from his hand. He broke into the attic, he turned over the rooms downstairs, and the outbuildings too, but his wife had fled. In her horror she had left even her child. The Keeper went to it, and looked down on it as if to kill it where it lay. Rather, he seized the child roughly by the arm so that the blankets fell away and the blood from his own wounds fell over the tiny kicking body. He groped his way back to the Dish, half blind with the pain of his crushed face, even though the moon still rode high and though there were traces of the dawn away in the east.

All the while he had the child with him, pulling it through the brambles as he fell, letting it drop to the forest floor as he stumbled away from the cottage of carnage he had left behind him.

Chapter X

Long before the mayhem had burst over Mossymere cottage, the dog fox had returned to his dying home. At each of the gates now blocked to him, he had snuffled first, then pawed and finally dug frantically at the dry soil. Always the logs defied him though, through the sand he could hear his vixen's faint calls to him. His panic mounted in an answering whine. He fell to his belly and bit and pulled with his teeth. He scratched with his claws: every muscle in his body ached and yet nothing moved around the earth's entrances. A trap snapped over his brush but he wheeled and gnawed himself loose. For an agonised while his efforts were no more than the wind that blows the leaves over a grave though his silhouette rose and fell ceaselessly against the beam of the moon as he worked. His dervish shadow sat still at last.

He cocked his fine head and the black nostrils worked on the smallest of breezes. He strained every nerve of his tingling, taut-tuned body and above the barricade of one entrance he whiffed the escaping gas. He traced a crack in the soil with his paw and the gush of the poison grew into a steady flow. Once again, he dug with both fore and hind paws and the hairline fissure widened out. The gas now gulped at him in full flood. The fox's eyes welled and his head spun round and around the giddy stars, but he worked on with a crying desperation. A primary claw ripped back against a fist-sized flint and snapped away clean at the bone. His pads were shredded by the coarseness of the soil and he had to chew at the last of the trees' fibres and branches once his leg muscles had all but gone. Even then, he rallied and scraped with his back legs and the gas threatened to overwhelm his biting, chewing head as it gnashed over the ever enlarging hole.

His body was half through now, pushing, squirming, writhing into the earth itself. He twisted and he turned, and he near crushed his ribs, but at last his severed brush disappeared down beneath the soil. First he pulled clear his vixen but back and again he went for the brood of cubs. Each one he laid on the sand outside, avoiding the Keeper's traps with all his old ease. There was some breath in them all, in all three little brown rags that gulped and bit out at the night air. As each young one stirred, the dog pulled the cub up the wall of the Dish to lie hidden safe in the bracken jungle above. And when his job was done, the fox lay down in exhaustion, to watch and to lick the warmth back into his stirring coughing brood. Time that had stopped and had paused, almost, to watch, lurched on a pace and the wood became wild again with the return of the Keeper.

His swaying figure apeared in the growing light and he cracked open the dawn with his curses. A bloodied bundle lodged beneath his arm, a gun still warm over his shoulder as he blundered into the Dish. He burst the bracken before him and he smashed his way to the fox's earth. For ominous minutes there was silence, then a scream and very soon a shot that echoed around the Dish like a rock dropped into a previously sleeping pool.

Chapter XI

Gunfire, the rim of the rising sun and the day of the Lengthsman all coincided. He was then a man slipping towards middle age, full-bearded and rough enough to be taken for a tramp today. His trousers were of coarsest cloth, his boots ever crusted in the mud of the domain's tracks and rutted pathways and his jacket could have been snatched from any passing scarecrow. He never went hatless, without that hat that had been soaked and dried and shrunk and stained and ripped and torn until all the body was out of it and it lay limp as a gutted animal on his head. But there was more than this sepia image to such a man, the roadmender of the estate.

The upkeep of his 'length' of these miles of causeway and pot-holed track was a service that never could be completed: the highway never ends but joins on to his brother and so the Lengthsman's white road stretched forever into the distance and his life crabbed eternally around the twin orbs of the estate and of the seasons as unchanging as the sun's path in the skies above him. Thus was the hero of ethereal patience of eternal dedication. He was something grander than a ditcher, more of an engineer, plotting the dips and the cambers of the roads and digging the peaty cuttings to drain off the dips. He was a hand scyther, cutting back the thistle, nettle, bracken and dogrose that tumbled over the lanes after a summer storm. The wet, heavy brocade of vegetation was home to the flies that savaged his hands and pumped them with venom until the skin stretched as smooth and shining as blue-veined porcelain. He was painter too, daubing in white the milestones to worlds he would never visit. Come spring he filled the frost wounds and became stone crusher with hammer, pick and barrow.

He worked six days every week, every daylight the season sent him and he knew both weeks of solitude and hours of companionship. He was a friend of the gypsies on their seasonal migrations and of all the other wanderers of those poorer days. He talked with the pedlars and the tramps, with the children dawdling on their way to school, the labourers slow on their path to work and the cowman taking his loves to the market. From the November rains, the period of great quietness set in. It stretched from the last leaf-fall to the gale days of January and into the bleak weeks of February when the clouds were low and the people of the estate hid like mice in their nests in the earth. Often it could snow for weeks and though his feeble paths blew in with each fresh night's storm, he was out again at dawn. He never let go and, sometimes, was rewarded with treasure: a guinea on the main drive, a silver petrol cap on the verge of the grand road they called the Sovereigns and even a baby that morning in the Devil's Dish.

CHAPTER XII

Following the sound of that single shot, the Lengthsman passed the cottage and he stayed there a long while searching for the young wife and her baby. He went through all the rooms and traced the signs of violence outside around the garden and into the thicket scrubs, but he found neither bodies nor witnesses to what had taken place. So, once again, he set off down the avenue of trees towards the Dish. At the moment of gunfire, the buzzard out in the early dawn had spiralled away in alarm, but now the bird was back, hovering over the crater. From a distance he saw black against the sunrise, but as the Lengthsman drew near, he marvelled at the bird's transparency of feather in the strong light. And from two hundred feet this marbled butterfly of a bird saw the Lengthsman, a black shadow on the ground, approach the rim of the Devil's Dish.

The man skirted the rim until he reached the pathway that the Keeper had forced down the side in his comings and his goings. He followed the track to the bottom of the pit where the sunrise hardly touched and the light was subdued and ominous. Across an oak branch a man lay, tumbledown, his head and shoulders slumped into the foliage around. The Lengthsman bent to a gun beside in the sand. The barrel was still warm and whiffed strongly of powder. He half turned the body with his boot, saw it was the Keeper and that his face was blown quite away.

The Lengthsman pushed the body away from him and retreated back across the floor of the Dish. His foot caught in a snare and pulled him over into the nettles. Thick sacking around his legs saved him from injury and he could ease off the noose and begin, slowly and carefully, to disengage all the traps and to slip the remainder of the snares. He buried deep into the sand a clutch of poisoned eggs around which the earliest bluebottles already lay, killed the instant they sucked. Cutting away a branch of elder, he poked around the mouths of what was the foxes' earth. The smell of decay and mingled gas was pungent still and traps closed firmly over the sticks at two of the entrances. The third that he found was reopened wide with a huge log rolled away down the incline.

The Lengthsman used his elder rod again and deep in the cavern of the earth struck something soft and yielding. After checking the sand around, the Lengthsman kneeled to the opening and with very great caution reached into the tunnel. He was as deep as his shoulder dreading the feel of some slaughtered animal, but, rather did he feel cloth and then a small, hairless body. The Lengthsman had found the baby, the wife's little girl. The child was barely alive. Sand caked her eyes, mouth and nostrils. Her breathing was laboured and faint. Her tiny naked limbs were numb with the early morning chill and her wispy-haired scalp was already bitten red by the fleas that infested the earth. The Lengthsman wrapped the child into his waistcoat and tucked her in the warmth of his armpit and hurried up from the darkness of the Dish's floor.

He struggled to the rim: dawn had become glorious morning. An unclouded sun was up over the cornfield and mist smoked oaks and the man lifted the child towards it as though to catch its warmth and power. As he washed the baby's face clean in the dew from the headland grasses, she at last began to cry, to move her hands, and to push away the folds of soiled pinstripe from her little body. Skylarks were singing as the Lengthsman in his new found life wandered down the ride again and away from that ugly place.

Part Four

The Mourner

CHAPTER I

Very early one morning I received a call, long distance the operator said, from a man who had found difficulty in reaching me. It was the Mossymere postman. He reported that he had found the house in chaos. There was no sign of Joe there but in the maelstrom of papers he had come across my name and number. He had not wanted to contact the police because, he said, Joe was a 'very irregular sort of chap' and there might yet be no need to 'wurrit'. I told him that he had shown great initiative, that he had done quite the right thing and that I would be there just as quickly as the roads to that rural place allowed. He replied that he would finish his round and meet me back in the wood in the mid to late morning.

My journey was hell: even at seven the Monday morning traffic around the city's orbital road was vicious. What little motorway there was out north soon became double carriageway and a final hundred miles of slow road behind dawdling country and farm traffic. I still clung to the hope that my presence at Mossymere would avert something terrible and every harvester, every little town traffic jam I saw as tilting the balance towards tragedy. My worry was not over Joe alone: I fretted constantly I should have told Jan and involved her in this desperate journey. Still, I knew that would have been a weakness I could not allow myself: his poor wife had suffered pain enough without this final stab. Nor could I deny some self interest: my investment in this ill-fated book had been substantial.

I possess a good memory for places visited and my drive down the last miles of ever-dwindling lanes was unerring. I found the track, unlocked the gate and I was into Mossymere, Joe's last, lost domain. I parked next to his car. Bracken grew up all around it and obviously he had not driven it for days. A van was also there in the small woodland clearing and an elderly man in uniform came to greet me.

'Thank goodness you're here at last, sir. I've been worrying no end the police should be called.' He showed me into the house – it was as he had said, badly thrown about. Wildly I asked him for news of Joe.

'Just don't know, sir. I've searched all about here. In the wood and all, but nothing. He hasn't been seen by no one in the village and not nowhere else as far as I've heard tell. It's a bloody mystery, it is, sir, I tell you straight.'

We agreed a coffee would be a good idea after such a long journey and to calm our nerves, to help us settle on some plan. We set about sorting the morass of photographs and notes that swamped the bare floor in the quest for some form of clue. And still, I quietly, fervently hoped Joe would walk in on us, surprised, content, even pleased to see me there.

Some of the photographs before me were brilliant. Perhaps a score I picked up and took to the light where I realised that there was a genius in Joe that had finally come close to materialisation. The difference between a fine photograph and one of brilliance is a slender one but in these Joe had bridged the intangible gulf. The lights were mesmeric and the forms so subtle that a thousand examinations would each find a different reward. But, sadly, many of the remainder were ordinary. Not a few were even slightly out of focus when he had not even taken the trouble to use a tripod at slow speeds.

The notes I gathered into some sort of order. Some were complementary to the work. Others explained the happenings between our last meeting and this unfortunate morning. Some of the scraps were drunken and barely made sense at all but I realised with a full comprehension how Joe's mental universe had been rocked by the events of these last few weeks. His despair at times was so obviously great that I could not believe he would not contact me. Or his wife. I was appalled that he had been content to be so abandoned.

Chapter II

'Sir,' the postman said abruptly, 'this envelope has your name on it.'

He had found it on the mantlepiece, quite apart from the other papers in the room. Inside the letter was clearly in Joe's handwriting but exceptionally hard to read. Indeed towards its end, it was all but illegible. Drink or sheer emotion had obviously unsettled him massively. After a couple of warm sentences referring to our long-time friendship, he continued.

'What a bastard of a night this has been. I've roamed the woods for hours. I just cannot explain what all this means to me. I simply cannot. You, of all people, know that this affliction of the heart has only struck me the once before with such intensity. Everything, absolutely everything I want is in her, around her – is her. For me there can be no solution without her. This is mad. I am unstable, but I was not before. You know that. I suffer from the mind-bending power of this sensation some people call love and I feel is something far more fundamental.

'Perhaps in some way I was vulnerable when I came here – you yourself spoke of my desire to drink the dregs of that damned youthful summer. Perhaps that fated me. And now I know Maggie's horror when she lost me. Once her, now I am the victim of a Mossymere passion.

'But what's the bottom line, eh, old friend? I cannot have

Swallow because I can only love her in the way I've known these weeks. She has made my life complete but now she has been wrenched away from me and, hope to God, in time to save her. I just never guessed. I beg you, believe me. I never knew about this relationship between us, though I curse my blindness, my lack of intelligence and investigation into the past. If I'd thought for a moment there could be the possibility we were indeed father and daughter then I would never ever have done this thing.

'You'll see Jan and tell her, please, that I am so sorry my weakness has led to this. She'll face so bravely so much more than I back away from now that every last fibre of me is ashamed. Old friend, so sorry to burden you with all this – at least you were in nearly from the start and I knew you'd have to be at the end. If they don't know yet, you'll find me in the Dish. There's not a lot of the book done, but if you can patch it up into anything, do your best. And let Jan keep the advance, eh, for old times' sake, please.

Yours ever,

Joe.'

CHAPTER III

I looked at the postman. 'The Dish?' I asked quietly.

'Oh my God, sir, he hasn't, has he?'

'I don't know any more than you. Not till we've been.' I remember him saying, 'Let's call the police. This ain't our job no more'. I fought a rising tide of panic. I am typical, after all, of the common herd which sees a crisis and ignores it, crosses the road, turns the eye, puts it far out of the mind. Why was I on this errand? I wondered, come to that, if I had ever really liked Joe – but I knew that at times I had been infatuated with him. This was fear most ignoble.

'Joe is my best friend and this is my job. I'll go alone, of course. You've done quite enough here already. Don't worry any more, just point me the way to follow.'

The good man, however, led me on the longest journey of my life. Every step of it I feared would be the last. The trek could not be far enough for me. I never wanted to see the end of the lush bracken and the stark larch trees. A pheasant cried out at us from another world where there was life and light outside this silent funereal corridor through the forest.

But we reached the Dish and for the first time I looked into the old quarry where I was so afraid my friend would lie. I still prayed that he had buckled under the pain of his discovery and left, gone, disappeared off to another existence and that I would not be the one to find him. Never in my life had I bargained for this. The path in the bracken was quite distinct: no longer could I postpone the search. The trail down was wildly irregular. I followed any number of false turnings and I realised how distraught the man had to be to push this maze before him.

On the floor of the Dish though I found my friend. His wrists were gashed again and again, I presumed with the dagger of glass that lay just outside his fingers. I stayed with his body a space and thought of his work, his life of loves that conquer all. Strong in my mind then was Jan, for love was something that she possessed in such quantity, so selfless, so unquestioningly given. All summer long I had believed that this would be enough, that their problems would blow themselves out, submerge, be quenched in this ocean of adoration. I had never thought that Joe could be blind to such a truth that even I could see and feel and warm to. I had always envied Jan's love for Joe. What would not I have done to be so cherished and yet this impulsive man beside me was capable of its utter denial. Even as I looked on Joe's cold body I still half believed that if Jan were to embrace it, to breath on it, to kiss it then fresh life would pump the veins. It was not the sight of Joe in his own blood but the image, then, of Jan, that brought my tears finally to start.

Chapter IV

With great sadness I retraced my path up the Dish side into the daylight. The postman stood there still, accompanied now by a girl. I knew at once who she was. Tall as the man beside her, dark haired, the girl of the photographs, she was the reality of Joe's crisis, the eye of his storm. Even as I cried, even in my utter despair at how this summer had ended, I found myself fascinated by her. She was indeed beautiful – a fact that I had not appreciated in Joe's work which I had looked at professionally and, I'll admit, cynically too. I had no way of knowing her feelings as she stood there that day: she was a pillar of calm.

'Denny has told me,' she said, 'and I see from your face that he's right.' She had a bicycle by her and a case strapped to its saddle. She caught my gaze, weighed its implication and continued. 'We were going away today. It was his idea. He told me only yesterday he would take me to the coast.' She looked away to the north. 'We were the far side of the wood, by the lake. He appeared so happy then. Only hours ago.'

Swallow was wearing a vivid dress. It was of deep red that set afire her black and chestnut hair and cloaked her body tight. I saw the fabric swell and fall ever more quickly as, I supposed, she struggled with the truth of the situation. Denny, I now knew the postman's name, stroked her hair as she laid her head on his shoulder.

'Rotten luck, sir. Rotten, rotten luck,' he repeated.

To be with Swallow made me at last realise the power of the Mossymere tale. I could now see something of why Joe had died, for hers was a body and a soul that any man would yearn to possess. And yet, even I could appreciate that never, not even in love and ecstasy, would he ever feel he had all of her, hold her totally or know all her physical or spiritual secrets. I believed that she herself had to be marked by this: she was the girl who would live with the memory of this summer for the rest of her life. This lost, abandoned girl – and at Joe's door surely lay the credit for her creation and her destruction both. I moved towards her, took her hand and pressing her cool skin, I hated my friend, his arrogant selfishness and his futile indulgences. His was a life paved with excuses and lies. He was a man incapable of satisfaction and to be with Swallow then made me half happy his body was at last at some kind of rest.

I wondered if she knew the truth, why Joe had really died. I felt I risked my very life as I spoke.

'I was Joe's best, oldest friend and so Swallow, believe me, none of this is down to you. He loved you. Really he did. All this horror is about other things.'

She just looked at me: right through me: words of Joe's came back to me: I too found her gaze, her brown eyes impossible to resist and I fell helplessly silent.

'Don't bother,' she said in a deep hushed voice. 'I know. I know everything, things that you do not realise.' She looked at me almost, I felt, with an emerging happiness. 'All this is to a plan,' she continued. 'Believe me, it was all fated. I've always known that Joe would come to Mossymere and that I'd be the one to keep him here.'

These words came from another era. They could not be this young girl's, with the glow of the sun around her. I looked at the ground, I remember, to establish some reality, but I doubted even the soil I stood upon. My whole conception of time and truth began to revolve around me. The bicycle had fallen. Swallow stood aloof from the postman who had been silent through this final episode. He was quite lost and I too winced. I was stabbed by shivers of the unknown; by fear of the Dish where my friend lay, by my awe of this girl his lover, his daughter, perhaps, of an affair with a long-dead mother. In turmoil, I let Swallow's lovely hand fall from mine.

CHAPTER V

I walked hurriedly to the house without any look backwards. I realised I had to call for the police and I picked up the stupid, old disconnected telephone. At once I threw it down in alarm and disgust. I sat a moment on the window sill but Denny had followed me in. To his question I said, 'You do that. I'd be grateful if you'd go and get them in for me now. And thanks for everything you've done.'

I settled down to sort the storm around: to file the notes, the pictures and to salvage what I could of Joe's last, at times, intensive work effort. Then I went through his cases of equipment, his cracked lenses, the filters strewn about and all the other evidence of treatment quite horrendous by a professional. I worked in a vacuum. I was half sickened by everything. I was seeing and hearing at one level but in reality I was both blind and deaf, kept alive alone by constant coffee and cigarettes. And still I was driven to make sense of it all for me, for Jan, for history even.

A figure appeared in the door. He introduced himself to me as the owner of the estate, Nicholas. I was surprised. He looked far more normal, far more workaday than anything Joe had said could lead me to expect. He appeared genuinely moved by the tragedy.

'Dennis has told me of this horrible thing and I have telephoned for the police. I warn you, they will be some time for we are a long way off their usual tracks. I can't tell you how sorry I am. I always believed Joe and I were close – or at least good friends. I am so sorry that he didn't think to get in touch with me rather than do this thing. I could have helped I'm sure. You won't know, but it's not the first tragedy this place has known. Back in Lordie's day a Keeper did away with himself here. It was before my time, but it always haunted Lordie – my father that was. I'd like to tell you I saw Joe only a few weeks back and he seemed quite normal to me. Stories had filtered through to me but the estate isn't used to any kind of artistic eccentricity after all. He looked tired perhaps, but we had a good long chat about the old days and the future too. I really am done about all this. It doesn't seem long ago he was first here and all those from that gang are gone. Maggie dead, Joe too and Ian moved away.'

'Ian is not here on the estate?' I asked startled.

'No, he's been long gone,' replied Nicholas.

'But surely Joe saw him this summer.'

'Not possible. He probably wished he had, though. They were very close the two of them in those days. And Maggie, of course. As I say, it's hard to believe they're all gone from Mossymere.'

We fell into a silence. He seemed to notice the afternoon was pulling in. 'Look,' he finished, 'come back to Swancoots when you're finished here. I reckon we could all do with some cheering up after all this.'

I accepted his offer with gladness.

Chapter VI

It was late in the afternoon when the police did arrive. Such was the silence of Mossymere that I heard their vehicle a long way off, scaring up a cloud of pigeons, startling pheasants along the track. They were full of excuses as they came up to me: finding the place had been difficult: they hardly knew the place existed even. In the end, a gardener from Swancoots had showed the final part of the journey and together in a desolate file we went up to the Dish. I led them down to the body and I remember how their young faces paled as they laid Joe's draping limbs on their stretcher. As they pushed a way back up the pit's side an arm splayed over the side and dragged in the bracken. I picked it up in my hand and held it until we reached the field above. I squeezed the fingers hard. I felt his wedding ring. I traced a long scar on the ball of his thumb from a wound he had received here twenty years before and which had never fully faded.

We were a sad procession from that hill, trailing down like a gallows party against the reddening sky. Back at the house they all left me whilst I made a last inspection there. I really did believe everything now at Mossymere was done. I packed my car with all Joe's possessions and drove away to meet Nicholas at Swancoots Hall.

Chapter VII

I was spellbound by the Hall in the quick, brilliant sunset of the late summer evening. I could quite see Joe's early excitement over it – now a most fantastical refuge after this most harrowing day of my life.

Nicholas himself welcomed me into a great stone hall and showed me along heavily panelled corridors to my room. It was vastly, incredibly medieval, granite walled and stone windowed. The furniture was from the very early modern period and there was a bathroom, probably late Victorian or Edwardian. The moat outside I watched catch the last of the sun as the swallows skipped its molten surface. I looked again and the bats were flickering in and around the roof turreting whilst the view now was shrouded in mist and shadows.

I met Nicholas in a vaulted drawing room, hung thickly with the portraits of his forbears. He offered me sherry and talked so sensibly that I could not believe but Joe was wrong about him. Joe was always capable of misjudging those in any type of authority. It was quite a block in him. He was even suspicious of me at times, I felt, as the provider of work. I felt he half despised me because I did not have sufficient talent to do it myself.

We moved into a dining room where a cold buffet awaited us. I realised how hungry I was and heaped my plate with fine white trout, from the river Nicholas said, and salad.

Wine was perfectly chilled. It was an excellent meal in every way. I mentioned the old poet, Herbert Walker, the man who had so influenced Joe as a student. To my surprise Nicholas looked utterly blank.

'Herbert Walker?' he said. 'There has never been anyone of that name on the estate in my time. I'd swear to that.'

'Surely Joe spent time with him when he was first here,' I pressed.

'I'm sure he didn't. Only with Ian and Maggie that I know of.'

I tried again. 'This Walker chap lived in a house by the river where the stream meets it.'

'There were gypsies in there then. And all of them quite young. There certainly was no poet then or since I assure you. And don't think I'm forgetful of that summer either. It made some impression on me as well as on your friend. I worried about the relationship between Ian and Joe and Maggie. It was all so intense. There was something very powerful between them all – a bond that grew and grew in the heat. It was a very hot summer, you remember? Always fine but for a couple of heavy storms. They were always together – Maggie even took to working on the harvester during the night shift though there was no need for it. Lordie tried to stop her. You couldn't have a woman working a twelve or fifteen hour day – but I believe they all needed each other. Ian's marriage was wrecked. Maggie was a lonely and desperate woman and Joe was young and vulnerable. If they weren't on the harvester then they'd all be out somewhere on the estate together. There was a lot of talk about them, of course, which didn't do Maggie any good. She'd always been treated as a bit of a "wrong 'un" as they say and the life she led with Ian and Joe didn't help her reputation. After all, she was nearly forty then you know? She died, poor woman, the year after Joe was here. Ian was devastated by it. We discussed making contact with Joe but as he had never returned we felt it best to let the past lie. And I didn't quite have the nerve to tell Joe at the start of his stay this time.'

'She died giving birth to Swallow then,' I said sadly.

Nicholas looked astounded. 'Who on earth told you that?' he exclaimed.

Once again I felt a void opening to receive me. I thought back quickly. 'Joe told me. It was in his story. In his notes.'

Nicholas sighed. 'I don't know what Joe was like outside Mossymere, but here his reason seems to have played a good few tricks on him. Swallow was a waif, taken in by Maggie's old widower. He took her in just like he'd cared for Maggie thirty odd years before. He's incredibly ancient now. He hasn't worked for decades and is quite gone in the head if you ask me.'

In the long silence that followed I looked searchingly at Nicholas. I could see no reason for him to lie and yet his interpretation of Mossymere's tragedies rang so different to Joe's. History, I knew, is no exact science: it is all tall story. The only fact here was the corpse of my long-time friend. I realised how tired the long day had left me and I was pleased to go up to my room.

Chapter VIII

I expected to fall asleep at once, but I could not. It was a still night with a bright moon that flooded across the ancient room and lay full over my bed. In the silence I heard voices from the day and from the past and could make little separation between them. I feared also for the morning when I had promised the police I would talk to Jan. They were breaking orders, but were humane enough to realise such news comes better from an old and trusted friend. Try as I might I could not escape her face.

Towards two perhaps, I left the bed and stood by the casement looking over the moat, the gardens, the silvered fields and towards Mossymere. The big wood loomed a dark slash against the gun barred night sky. It was fearful, full of menace, bringing me to shudder, forcing my thoughts to the absolutely real: which way should I approach the city for Jan's house? Should I telephone her to ensure she stayed in for me? The car's tank had been low and would I have petrol enough for the nearest market town? Could I make anything of Joe's last work to salvage his name and bring in useful money for his family? And while I thought all this I knew that I saw a light out there amongst the trees, burning bright from Mossymere. I knew it to be so. I entered the hallway outside my room and found that from there it shone clearer still. A lantern. A lamp. There was life out there in the forest.

I paced the floorboards, my feet cold on the oak. I flung open the windows to listen, but the stillness brought only silence. Was Swallow out there, alone, in despair? Was Ian come back to look for his friend? The Lengthsman was it, or some passing wayfarer as in days of old? My yearning was to return to bed, to forget, but my impulse was to follow the light, to trace the fantasy to its source. The clock tower chimed a silvery double note. It was half past two and I dressed.

The beams of the ancient house creaked around me and rooms breathed to the ticking of clocks and the slumber of ancient oak. The stairway was alive, rippling like the planking vessel in a storm. Outside the door a cat howled and spat. There was a low growl from the dogs in their run. I followed the moat, solid mercury under the moon but for where a toad splashed and eddied black. I passed a small copse where a hunting owl called me back. Then I was over the meadows, hardly dressed for the cold that grew ever more piercing as the wood closed. I brushed past sheep feeding on the marsh pasture and could not deny how the chill inside me grew every step.

Mossymere was all around me. I stood still some minutes. The Swancoots clock chimed three, but that was the only sound and I moved on to where the trees towered and the lamp still burned. Over the cottage garden the light glowed on the wilderness. And again I paused; afraid of the memory; frightened of the tale that I have told; but remembering how to admit fear to oneself is to run from it forever. And so I continued on.

Chapter IX

The door was ajar as if to receive me. I knocked and called out my name but as I spoke the lamp died. My way in was lit by the moonbeams. I stepped into the kitchen and then into the main room but as I walked the panic in me dissolved. I could actually feel it abandon me. I grew warmer. I touched the lamp and though it was cold, I did not care, nor find it strange. I had seen its light and that was fact enough for me. Now, in this strange circumstance, for the first time I was not afraid of the Mossymere house.

There was softness everywhere in the air. I even imagined the shattered clock to tick for me. I believed that Joe was close then, and though his body was gone, his spirit was around me in the domain that he had always sought. No decay would touch him now. He could be here, happy with his past for eternity.

I recalled Nicholas's words, that they were always together, and Maggie's letter too from twenty years past. 'So happy together,' she had written. And, as I remembered, the pain of the house had vanished for me until even the moon outside seemed to wear the smile of a broad genial face. Joe's desertion those years back was at last forgiven. His soul was where it belonged and the scars inflicted by his departure were beginning to heal.

It was fanciful of me, but I sensed peace around. And certainty. All my distress had been laid in those few minutes. I felt at last that I had the final ending of the tale begun so long ago. And so it was that I wanted everything to be for my friend. Fearing to break the spell, I left Mossymere and then Swancoots that very hour.

I wrote Nicholas that I wished to avoid the early morning traffic but in truth, I did not wish my final conclusion to be disturbed. For, I tell you, in the end, I am above all else a realistic man. There is nothing about Mossymere that has not disturbed me beyond reason and I simply rejoice that with this last sentence my association with it can reach a final ending.